HIDDEN TRIBES OF INDIA

ACKNOWLEDGMENTS

This book would not have been published without the support and help of the following people to whom we owe our warmest thanks.

Foremost, we should like to thank our editor who believed in our project, the Indian government and all the local authorities who permitted us to enter protected areas and those closed to foreigners.

We should especially like to thank Mr Prem Prashant, Director of the Ministry of Home Affairs in New Delhi, Mr Dera Natung, Minister of Information, Public Relations and Tourism in Arunachal Pradesh, Dr M.M. Kutty Ias, Deputy Commissioner of Tawang, Mr T.S. Randhawa, Mr D. Mishra, S. Norbu Phaichelupa and L. Dawa.

We should also like to thank Tapas Kar, F.P.O. of Tawang, SMITI Ruby Yabiyang, Rinchin Dorje, S.C.O. of Bombdila and the museum staff, Rajendra Singh Kushwaha, Maharaja Udaiveer Singh of Banswara for his hospitality during the Bhil festival in Rishabdeo, the Maharaja and Maharanee of Wankaner and Mr Gaurishanker, K.C. Draval from Anjar and Dinesh K. Vyas D. M. in Mundra.

We are particularly grateful to our friend Ayesha Lumba whose collaboration was invaluable in bringing this project to fruition.

We should also like to thank and express our regards for Malika Sarabhai, Bipin Shah and Mrinalini Sarabhai for their hospitality and valuable help; Barry Underwood for the information he provided us with on the Bhils; Rahe Shyam Agarwal of Muniguda who was our guide and interpreter with the Kandhas; and Satya Nanda and Hussein for the help and support they gave us among the Bondas and other Orissa tribes.

Thanks also to Motiram Vadu and Mona Mehta, Jiribai Naryan, Charibai Karsan, Bikkha Deva Jever, Maganbhai T. Bhatti, Mohmand Hussein, Krishman Kutty Nair, Yasu Pal and Gulbeg Singh, and David C. Wanniang.

Our thanks go to our friend Blagang Dada – and his family – who zealously guided us on the river and hillside paths of the Nishi country.

We also thank the group of Nishi students in Seppa.

We are eternally grateful to Jatanlal Bucha and his children for his hospitality in Guwahati and the help they brought us in time of need.

Our thanks equally go to Marie Renault and to Philippe Pierrelée who, with his creativity and professionalism, was instrumental in the successful completion of this work; we are also grateful for the sensitivity and friendship he showed us during the three years prior to this book's publication.

It remains for us to thank all those who welcomed us in their villages and let us photograph their daily life. Without their understanding and assistance this book would not have been possible.

Lastly, warmest thanks to our friends Giovanni and Cristina for all their encouragement.

TIZIANA AND GIANNI BALDIZZONE

Jacket: *Nishi warrior (Arunachal Pradesh)*
Endpaper: *Painted tiger-dragon at Tawang Monastery (Arunachal Pradesh)*

HIDDEN
TRIBES
OF INDIA

Tiziana and Gianni Baldizzone
Preface by Dominique Lapierre

Text by
Declan Quigley and
Vinay Srivastava

Local Colour

CONTENTS

Characteristic hairstyle of the Bonda tribe (Orissa).

PREFACE

India — the oldest civilisation in the world. A landmass with a population of nearly a thousand million. A mosaic of peoples, races, cultures, religions and languages of unmatched richness and diversity. A nation full of contrasts and separate worlds such as those of the tribal peoples to which this magnificent book pays worthy tribute. Today the native inhabitants number over 40 million. Some of their ethnic groups, such as the Gonds and the Bhils of central India or the Santals and Khasis of Assam were the first people to populate the country ten or 20 thousand years ago.

Progressively driven back towards the mountainous and forested areas by the thrust of invasions, for a long time they lived on the fringe of Indian society. Pure children of nature, supremely free beings, through the ages they have expressed their exuberance, purity and vivid character in the completely original and abundant manifestations of their culture. They represent a precious part of man's heritage and, to this end, they deserve our support, respect and recognition.

By revealing to us particularly stimulating aspects of the Adivasi civilisations, Declan Quigley and Vanay Srivastava's text and Tiziana and Gianni Baldizzone's photographs enrich our knowledge of this little known vibrant reality of the Indian landscape. During my research for *The City of Joy*, I had the honour of meeting an Adivasi family in one of Calcutta's shanty towns. After weeks of patient attempts to overcome their shyness, I was able to reconstruct the journey that had led the forest dwellers to exchange their mountainous jungle for anonymity in the maze of a shanty town slum. A pitiful and typical journey which illustrates the difficult situation millions of India's aboriginals face today. One morning, two hundred henchmen sent by the local landowners swooped like a flock of vultures on the wooded valley where Bouddhou Koujour and his tribe lived at the borders of Hihar and Madhya Pradesh states. Having set fire to the huts, they demanded back rents and interest on loans, arrested the men with the help of the police, siezed the cattle, raped the women and plundered the tribe's possessions. The raid represented the culmination of several centuries of clashes between ancestral peoples inhabiting the forest and the powerful landowners who laid claim to their fields and harvests. An ancient law recording the wish that the jungle belong to he who cultivated it should have protected my Adivasi friend and his tribe from these covetous desires. At first nomadic, then seminomadic, in due course they had become small-time farmers cultivating food crops to feed their families. The natural resources of the forest served to complete their harvest's yield.

Koujour and his family told me how parents and children would climb the trees and pick the berries, how they scratched away the earth to uncover edible roots. They knew how to strip off certain barks, peel tubers and extract the flesh, press leaves with curative properties, find edible mushrooms, collect tasty lichen, extract sap, gather buds and harvest wild honey. They would set snares and springs, place nooses and nets for small game, and prepare automatic clubs or arrow traps to ensnare bears and other large animals. They would catch insects, gather worms and hunt ants' eggs and giant snails. Everybody gave the surplus of his catch to the group for the old people, the widowed, the orphans and the sick. "It was a hard life, but we were free and happy."

Like the other families in the valley, Bouddhou Koujour had to leave his land behind. He sought work in several regions, then was lucky enough to find shelter in the Calcutta slum. That day, India was shamed: a shanty town had absorbed men who personified the essence of Man, primitive and free.

Bouddhou Koujour's story is but one example of the great drama lived by India's hidden tribes today. Everywhere tribal culture is disappearing, which is what makes this book a testimony of untold value. The decline of the Adivasis is nothing new. For generations, these people of the forest lived in fear, but until recently their inaccessible haunts afforded them relative protection. The massive deforestation which is destroying their habitat and depriving them of their traditional means of subsistence, improved communications, urbanisation and the determination of the central government to integrate fringe populations into the economy are all factors that are progressively causing the tribal peoples to lose their indentity. Despite the many privileges and guarantees they were granted by the Indian constitution after independence in 1947, the living conditions of most Adivasi have barely improved. In many cases, they have deteriorated immensely.

Deprived of a decent living from the land and heavily exploited by traders and powerful landowners, many tribal peoples have been forced into the industrial centres to become workers, which means traumatic exile as one cannot undo in one generation, customs that are centuries or even hundreds of centuries old. An exile which, in time, brought about the loss of their culture and traditions. The young Paites of the Kuki tribes in the Manipur Valley between Assam and Burma no longer know how to weave the magnificent naturally dyed cloth that was once the pride of the fashionably dressed in Bombay and Calcutta. The intrusion of television cameras has virtually destroyed the livelihood of the Dewars, nomadic bards who travelled throughout the country playing and singing their repertoire of glorious folklore. Forced to abandon their livelihood, they now have to set up their bamboo camps at the edge of towns and rummage through dustbins and pick over rubbish to make a living as ragmen. I could quote plenty of other examples.

Despite commendable attempts so far, will the Indian government some day manage to shield the tribal peoples from their unjust fate? It is sincerely to be hoped. Sadly, the causes of this curse run deep. The economic and social development of these minority communities clashes with the powerful interests of those who continue to gain substantial profits from their long-standing exploitation. Particularly traders, profiteers and, more generally, those in key positions who, over the years, have made their fortunes from the misery of others, all vehemently oppose the course of justice. Even more serious, as victims of historical exploitation, many Adivasi have now lost hope of seeing their condition improve. A general pessimism, not to mention profound fatalism, has seized many of these men and women for whom life has always been precarious. Some forsake their own well-being and simply wait for help from the state. For others, the only hope of justice is in violence and revolt. Numerous trouble spots mark today's ethnographic map in India, tensions which add to other explosive factors and threaten the unity of the country. But above all, these forgotten peoples wish to be recognised for what they are. Are they not entitled to this? Are they not rightfully and have for so long been part of the essence of India? Are they not a piece of the history of this great, ancient land?

Dominique Lapierre

INTRODUCTION

Tribal India is virtually unknown to the outside world and, surprisingly, also to millions of Indians in both the towns and countryside who go about their daily lives completely oblivious of their "neighbours" in the deserts and mountains.

This book captures a glimpse of that hidden India. Although accounts of a few tribal groups by travellers and anthropologists are available, virtually nothing is known about many other communities. Anthropologists, as well as the Indian media, have tended to focus on the large, politically powerful tribal groups while the smaller communities have been largely ignored. They deserve our attention as their existence is threatened by every contact with the "developed" world, whether with local money-lenders, government planners concerned with their development, or tourists. Even a book such as this is a kind of intrusion, but we hope that our account, through text and photographs, shows the tribes of India as they themselves would want to be seen.

Tribes have been defined as isolated or semi-isolated communities. With well-demarcated territory, political autonomy and a cultural system, dialect, folklore and deities of their own, they are groups with a sense of separate identity. However, they are not always as isolated as they appear to be, for tribes throughout history have interacted with each other and with other non-tribal people.

Growing encroachment by outsiders on tribal territories in the forests and hills has pushed the tribes further and further back into the interior. This has in many areas produced a strong sense of tribal identity. The tribes claim that they were the first settlers of the land that they inhabit and justify their right over land, natural resources, forests and water through their myths of origin.

Tribal communities have over the years been referred to by value-loaded and pejorative terms such as "primitive", "savage", "exotic", "barbarian", "naked", "uncivilised" and so on. Today, however, there is a growing realisation that people who are different from ourselves are equally worthy of

respect, and that such stereotyped and preconceived notions of them should be avoided.

Over the last century or so the way of life of Indian tribes has been subject to many changes. A variety of occupational groups have emerged, and education has weakened some traditional customs and practices. But the sense of belonging to the tribe has normally remained firm. This has important implications in the modern political arena where tribes have been banding together to fight for their common interests.

The Indian government uses the official term "Scheduled Tribes" to designate tribal populations. According to the 1981 census of India, these groups account for 7.76 per cent of the total population. They are broadly concentrated in the following regions of India:

The Himalayan Region — A great many tribal groups can be found in the mountain valleys of northeastern India. These include groups such as the Apa Tani, Adi, Nishi, Garo, Khasi, Kuki, Mismi and Naga. In the sub-Himalayan regions of Bengal, Uttar Pradesh, Himachal Pradesh and Sikkim live other tribes such as the Bhotia, Raji, Lepcha, Rabha and Zanskari.

Central India — This area covers parts of the states of Bihar, Orissa, Madhya Pradesh, and West Bengal, and the tribes living here include the Kandha, Bhumji, Gond, Ho, Oraon, Munda, Santal, Saora and Paraja.

Western India — Several tribal communities including the Bhil, Saharia, Mina and Rabari live in the states of Rajasthan, Maharashtra, Gujarat and Goa.

Southern India — This region includes the states of Karnataka, Andhra Pradesh, Tamil Nadu and Kerala. The tribes called Toda, Badaga, Irula, Kurumba and Kota all live in the Nilgiri Hills. Other important tribal groups in

Prepared for the name-giving ceremony, this child will recieve her new name from the tribe's shaman.

the south include the Gonda, Chensu, Mala Malasar and Kadar.

The Indian Ocean Islands — On the Andaman and Nicobar Islands to the east and Lakshadweep Island to the west can be found several other tribal groups – the Great Andamanese, Sentinel, Shompen, Onge, Jarwa and Car Nicobarese.

Inhabiting almost ever region of India and divided into nearly 461 communities (including 174 sub-tribes), according to the Peoples of India project, the "Scheduled Tribes" differ widely in demographic and cultural features. There are very large tribes like the Bhil (7,367,973 people), Gond (7,449,193), Santal (4,260,842), Oraon (1,871,995) and Mina (2,087,075), while at the other extreme there are those tribes with a population of less than 100 (like the Great Andamanese who number only 42, or the Onge who were estimated to number only 97 in 1984).

Racially also, the Indian tribes fall into different categories: the tribes of central India mostly belong to the Proto-Australoid group; those of the sub-Himalayan and eastern frontiers have Mongoloid characteristics; the Kadar of south India and the tribes of the Andaman Islands are believed to have racial affinities with African negros.

Inhabiting different parts of India, the tribes have developed (and sometimes acquired) many different languages. Some northeastern tribes speak dialects which are related to Chinese or Burmese while those communities that claim to have migrated from Tibet, or have traded with Tibetan merchants, speak Tibetan dialects. The central Indian tribes speak Austro-Asiatic languages, while those in the south speak several different Dravidian dialects. Tribes that are spread over different states have gradually adopted the dominant language of the region in which they live. For example, the Rabari in Haryana and Pubjab speak Hindi or Punjabi, those in Rajasthan speak Marwari, while those living in Kutch speak both Kutchi and Gujarati. The Bhil are a distinctive exception to this pattern, retaining their original dialect notwithstanding their distribution across different states.

The tribes differ widely in their social and cultural practices. The Khasa of Jaunsar-Bawar (Uttar Pradesh) are polyandrous (i.e. one woman has more than one husband), while the Apa Tani (Arunanchal Pradesh) are polygynous (i.e. one man has more than one wife). The Garo and Khasi of Meghalaya are distinctive in being matrilineal (i.e. they trace their ancestry along the mother's line). More commonly, however, tribal societies are patrilineal, the Bhil being a good example of a community where patriliny is greatly valued. There are other groups, such as the Gaddi of Himachal Pradesh and the Rabari of Gujarat and Rajasthan, where women play a very important role in decision making although these societies are basically patrilineal. Among the Rabari, women are responsible for all commercial activities, whether selling milk and clarified butter to local people, or traditional costumes and wall-paintings to tourists.

Similarly, there is wide variation in the economic practices of the tribes. The hill tribes in the northeastern and central regions of India depend on shifting cultivation. The larger tribal groups, such as the Santal, Gond and Bhil, are agriculturalists who have much in common with Hindu peasants. The Kadar, the tribes from the Andaman Islands, and the Chenchu of Andhra Pradesh still depend on hunting and food gathering. The Gaddi and the Gujar of Himachal Pradesh and the Toda of the Nilgiri Hills are pastoralists, while the Rabari specialise in camel breeding. But most tribes, it should be said, combine a variety of economic activities.

One of the identifying characteristics of a tribe is its religion. In general, because of the tribes' closeness to nature, the deities and spirits that enter into their religious systems are deified forms of natural phenomena. Thunder, lightning and rainfall, for example, are worshipped as gods, as are the sun and the moon, which some anthropologists say are universally worshipped among Indian tribes. But this does not mean that none of the tribes have a concept of an omnipresent, omniscient and omnipotent deity. The Bhil, for example, believe in a deity called Bhagwan who is thought to regulate the entire universe, and is referred to by many epithets, including "the true master", "the pious one", "the good and righteous one", and so on. Similarly, for the Bonda, there is a supreme being called Mahaprabhu. However, some students of tribal culture feel that the idea of an abstract, supernatural being has penetrated tribal cosmologies only because of their interaction with Hindus.

Early anthropologists often described a tribal belief in the existence of a soul animal in every natural phenomenon. Thus rivers and rainbows, mountains and boulders, the sun and the moon are regarded as living beings in the sense that humans are. In the censuses of India published before India's independence in 1947, tribal religion was classified as "soul worship" or "animism". The distinction between animate and inanimate found in Western thought is completely alien to them. The tribes also believe that their dead ancestors continue to exercise influence over their lives.

An Apa Tani woman (Arunachal Pradesh).

Many early observations of tribal religion remain relevant today. However, they tended to conceive of tribal society as completely self-contained, and in doing so failed to see the strong influence of external belief systems. Christianity, for example, had already made its impact felt on the Angami and Ao Naga by the mid-19th century. As early as the 1860s, C.D. King was working as a missionary among the Angami of Kohima.

In 1952 the government appointed a Tribal Welfare Committee that divided the tribes into four categories:

Tribal Communities — who confine themselves to their original habitats and follow traditional patterns of life. These have suffered the most because of encroachments on their territories by outsiders.

Semi-tribal Communities — who have more or less settled down in rural areas by taking to agriculture and other allied occupations. By living among Hindus, who are divided into different castes, the tribes have also come to be regarded as separate castes and have adopted the concepts of purity and pollution associated with caste.

Acculturated Tribal Communities — who have migrated to urban or semi-urban areas and are now working in industry and government organisations.

Assimilated Tribes — who have been completely absorbed into the wider world and have thus effectively become detribalized.

Development in various sectors of Indian society has been co-ordinated through a number of "Five Year Plans", the first of which was launched in 1952. Each of these has had a special allocation of funds for tribal development and the results of every plan have been carefully scrutinized. In the fifth and sixth Five Year Plans (1972 and 1979), it was observed that since the tribes were so dissimilar, it was a mistake to have a uniform development policy. In practice, the benefits of such development policies favour the large, politically powerful tribes at the expense of the smaller ones. Statistics have also shown that the population of certain communities have been decreasing rapidly because of their weak political and economic position, and because of declining health and nutritional standards.

The government therefore, decided to prepare a list of the "lowest layer" among the "Scheduled Tribes" on the basis of four criteria: decreasing or near-constant population, pre-agricultural economy, extremely low level of literacy and a general state of social backwardness. These groups were called "Primitive Tribes" and were made the targets of intensive developmental programmes. There are currently 74 such tribes, including the Kadar (of Kerala), the Baiga and the Saharia (of Rajasthan and Madhya Pradesh), the Bonda (of Orissa) and the tribes of the Andaman and Nicobar Islands, all of whom have been extensively studied by anthropologists.

Attempts by the British administration to "civilise" the tribal populations resulted in radical changes. During British colonial rule, tribes lost a large portion of their land to outsiders because, being illiterate, they were unable to take advantage of British courts. The opening of mines in many tribal areas also brought a great deal of disruption to local populations. In Assam and southern India, tea, coffee and rubber plantations were established in tribal areas, and these, while offering employment to tribe members, usually exploited them.

With the opening up of the tribal homelands, there was also an influx of landlords and moneylenders who tacitly enjoyed the patronage of local officials. Tribal land was usurped and the people made to work as serfs or bonded labourers, their local institutions and customs condemned or derided. Often, however, the tribes revolted against their conditions and the cultural domination that accompanied them.

Along with the colonisers came missionaries who settled in many tribal areas. In tribal Bihar, the missionaries first confined their activities to evangelical work, but were not very successful. But once they began to help the tribes protect their land rights against outside interests by representing them in the courts, their mission thrived. Over the years indigenous tribal religions in some parts of India have been replaced by one or other denomination of Christianity.

The missionaries also established schools in which English was used as the principal medium of instruction. At the same time they introduced Western medical practices that supplanted the traditional healing systems. Indigenous lifestyles and ways of behaviour also underwent changes. Among the most conspicuous innovation was the abandonment of traditional dress, especially by men.

To prevent tribal societies from being exploited by outsiders, Verrier Elwin, the distinguished anthropologists, suggested, the creation of "tribal reserves" in which no outsider would be permitted to acquire land or open a business. Only when these areas were administratively

An old Monpa Man (Arunachal Pradesh).

protected, he argued, could the tribes be protected from exploitation by outsiders. Among Elwin's suggestions were the following: tribal councils should be established and they should adjudicate all conflicts; tribal leaders should not be used as government agents; missionaries and other religious zealots should not be admitted to tribal areas; non-tribals entering tribal areas should require licences; and no official should ever be stationed in tribal areas.

Elwin's approach was seen by many as isolating tribal societies, and was vehemently criticised by those who favoured the assimilation of tribes into mainstream Indian society. The supporters of assimilation thought that anthropologists were interested in keeping the tribes as they were so that they could study their customs in what was effectively an "anthropological zoo". This was certainly not Elwin's intention, which was simply to save tribes from exploitation.

The problems facing tribes have multiplied since Elwin's day, and the worst affected are the small tribes. The bigger groups have been able to exert a certain amount of pressure on the government for a better deal. It has also been evident that politically powerful tribes have exploited the less powerful ones. With the exercise of total control over forests and other natural resources by the state and central governments, the traditional rights of tribes have been abrogated. Shifting cultivation has been prohibited and this has had unfortunate consequences in the areas where tribes have refused to take to plough cultivation.

Approximately 87 per cent of the tribes now live by agriculture and recognition of their land rights is therefore essential for their development. Traditionally, lands and forests were owned collectively by tribal groups but the Indian state does not recognise such rights. For groups living in the forests, between 30 and 50 per cent of their income comes from the collection of forest products, so it is obviously crucial that their access to these natural resources is not made illegal.

Development projects also often bring great disruption to tribal groups. For example, to provide more advanced irrigation systems, it is often necessary to build huge dams in or around tribal areas and this means that the local population has to be moved elsewhere. Of the 1.1 million people displaced by government development projects in recent years, nearly half belong to tribal groups. The World Bank estimated that around two million tribes people were facing problems of resettlement. In theory, people who are displaced in this way are supposed to receive adequate compensation in order to set up homes elsewhere. But many, including cattle breeders, hunters and food gatherers, shifting cultivators, landless artisans and farm works, never receive any compensation because they cannot prove ownership of the land from which they have been evicted.

Compensation usually takes the form of money. Since, most tribes are not used to dealing with cash, they often squander it recklessly and find themselves left with nothing. Sometimes they are given other sites, but more often than not the land is of very poor quality and it may also be very far from their place of origin, causing a deep sense of alienation. Sometimes displaced tribes move to towns and cities where they end up working as domestic servants, street vendors, rickshaw pullers, or unskilled labourers. Displacement of this kind destroys their institutions and their cycle of festivals and rituals.

The Indian government has given priority to protecting tribes from any sort of outside exploitation. For example, several laws have been enacted to halt the loss of tribal land. The state has also designated some tribal areas as "protected" and "reserved" and outsiders have been debarred from setting up any business in them. The Government made efforts to preserve the diversity of tribal cultures by protecting and promoting tribal languages, arts and crafts, songs, music and dance. In the following pages we will explore some of this extraordinary tribal diversity. One can only hope that it will continue for a long time to come.

A Nishi woman crosses a bamboo bridge (Arunachal Pradesh).

HEIRS OF THE HUMAN DAWN

Ethnologists have still not reached agreement about who inhabited India before the arrival of Caucasians (Aryans) from Central Asia over 2,000 years ago. The most widely accepted view is that the original inhabitants (or aborigines) of India were the tribes who were driven into thickly forested areas as the invaders began to colonise the land. Leading an isolated existence, the tribes of central and eastern India were long able to preserve their lifestyles. Only now, with the encroachment of commercial frontiers and the implementation of development plans by government and other agencies, have these traditional lifestyles begun to disappear. Nevertheless, some tribes still cling to their traditional ways and, among them, the tribes of Orissa are an outstanding example. This chapter deals with the Bonda, Gadaba and Koya tribes, the shifting cultivators of Orissa. These tribes are principally concentrated in Koraput district where they make up one-third of the total population.

The Bonda (or Bondo) call themselves Remo, which means "men". Ethnologists describe them as an example of the Austro-Asiatic racial strain in India. They inhabit the mountainous regions to the northwest of the Mauchkund River. What makes them distinct from the other tribes of Orissa is their language and customs, particularly their tendency to indulge in homicidal disputes (on which Verrier Elwin has written extensively). Their native dialect is a branch of the Austro-Asiatic family of languages, but in recent years they have become conversant with Oriya,

Old woman of the Gadaba tribe (Koraput region, Orissa).
OPPOSITE PAGE: *Young Bonda woman (Jeypore region, Orissa).*

the state language of Orissa which is of Indo-Aryan origin, which they use in their interaction with other tribes of the plains.

Earlier authors regarded the Bonda as a branch of the Gadaba, a much larger neighbouring tribe with similar racial and cultural characteristics. Edgar Thurston (1909) confused the matter by classifying them as Poroja (or Paraja), another tribe of Orissa, on the one hand, and describing them as a section of the Gadaba, on the other. Furer-Haimendorf (1945) demonstrated that the Bonda and Gadabad are independent tribes and that it is wrong to treat the former as a branch of the latter. They speak mutually incomprehensible dialects, although they belong to the same family of languages. In spite of the relationship that exists between them, each considers itself to be a separate unit in certain important ways. While both the Bonda and the Gadabad believe that the tribes of the entire area are one family, in matters of marriage, each is endogamous (i.e. does not permit marriage with outsiders).

The origin and affiliations of the Bonda are obscure. According to one of the their myths of origin, they are descended from one of the 12 Gadaba brothers who were born on the banks of the Godavari River and migrated from there to the Jeypore Hills in Orissa. Furer-Haimendorf (1945) describes them as belonging to the large group of Austro-Asiatic people who in Neolithic times developed an advanced and complex culture. This culture was characterised by worship of stone deities, rice cultivation on terraced and irrigated fields, domestication of cattle for slaughter and sacrifice, the art of weaving and the erection of megaliths in the shape of menhirs, stone circles and dolmens. These traits survive among both the Bonda and Gadaba.

The Gadaba were the palanquin bearers of Orissa. At one time, they served the King of Bastar (a district in Madhya Pradesh). The meaning of the world *gadaba* is "a person who carries loads on his shoulders". In those days the tribal council forbade any Gadaba to ride a horse and the penalty for doing so was exile. Thurston's explanation of this rule is as follows: "The Gadabas . . . are palanquin-bearers and have the same objection to a rival animal as a cart-driver has to a motor car."

The Gadaba are divided into seven subgroups: Bada, Kollar, Kaleyi, Kapu, Ketani, Porangi and Jurumu. The Kapu and Ketani have developed more, because they live close to the plains. The Gadaba subgroups are arranged in a kind of hierarchy. The highest in social status are the Bada Gadabas, who do not accept food and water from other lower groups. At the bottom of the hierarchy are the Kaleyi Gadaba, who are not allowed to sit with the other groups. However, the groups placed in the middle of the hierarchy intermix freely. These practices are similar to the Hindu caste system.

Geographically, the Bonda settlements can be divided into three groups: the Bara-jangar, the Gadaba and the Bonda of the plains. The Bara-jangar group are regarded as "pure" Bonda, and the twelve villages they inhabit are said to be the original Bonda settlements. The second Bonda group is called Gadaba because they have been influenced by the neighbouring Gadaba tribe. This is evident both from linguistic and material aspects of their culture. The Gadaba, for example, have taught them the art of making mats and baskets, and their language shows significant differences from that spoken in the Bara-jangar villages.

The Bonda of the Gadaba group do not acknowledge the authority of the headman (*naika*) of Mundlipada, the capital of Bonda land. They are also less interested in the cult of the Pat Khanda Mahaprabhu, which is very popular with the Bara-jangar. Festivals are observed by the two groups on different days. However, both the Bara-jangar and Gadaba Bonda inhabit the hills, and thus share the unit of hill dwellers vis-a-vis the plains dwellers.

The Bondas of the plains have been in close touch with caste Hindus for a long time and have consequently tried to eliminate those characteristics which mark them out in their neighbours' eyes as backward tribes. For example, in some of their villages, the women have grown their hair and pierced their noses for ornaments. The Bonda women of the hills, by contrast,

Young woman of the Gadaba tribe and her child (Koraput region, Orissa).
FOLLOWING DOUBLE PAGE: *Koya village in the ghats of Orissa.*

*Among the numerous tribes of Orissa and Andhra Pradesh, the horns of the bison
are an important part of the ceremonial costume.*
OPPOSITE PAGE: *A young woman with a characteristic Bonda hairstyle.*

shave their heads and wear ornaments in their ears, each ear being pierced in two places. But they never wear nose jewellery. The home-weaving industry, which is basic to Bonda existence in the hills, has been given up on the plains. Such changes have resulted in Hill Bondas looking down upon their counterparts on the plains. Marriages between the two hill groups are quite common, but unions between hill and plains tribes are very rare.

A Bonda village is not protected by a wall or a fence in spite of the incessant feuds between different settlements. Every village has a megalithic platform called a *sindibor*, which is the centre of their religious and social life. Nearby, there is often a shrine to a deity called Hundi. Sindibor is extremely important for Hill Bondas, and they criticise the plains dwellers for having abandoned him.

The Bonda house is self-contained. Each household contains two or more huts for the parents, the married sons and sometimes for other relatives of the family. A cattle shed and an open shelter where people sit to work and talk are essential elements of every house. The walls are of mud, with several wooden pillars supporting the roof, which is thatched with grass. The veranda is fenced with an unplastered bamboo wall. The whole edifice is slightly raised above the ground to keep out the rain. When a new house is constructed, the central pillar is erected first. The Bonda tie mango leaves around it to "bring the dead and the gods near".

The fenced-in veranda is used for grinding, husking grain, cleaning rice and millet, and weaving mats. Often, it also serves as a bedroom. The door of the hut opens into the first room where the people cook, sit and sleep. Above the hearth are two wooden trays, one over the other, for drying fish, meat, tobacco and new grain. In this room, an earthen platform is raised some 15 centimetres (6 inches) above the ground where pots of water, gruel and rice-beer are kept. The inner room serves as the granary room and a gourd, which represents the family deity, is also kept in it. Pigs and hens may both be housed in pens on the veranda, while a separate shed houses goats and cattle.

Since the Bonda do not observe menstrual taboos, they neither have an outhouse or a separate door for menstruating women, as is the case among the Gondas of Madhya Pradesh. Indeed, Bonda women, as Elwin (1950:122) writes, "have no idea of a public cloth".

Bonda society is organised into three different exogamous units, namely the village, the *moiety* (*bonso*), and the clan (*kuda*). The village is a sacred entity and the village boundaries are protected by magic rites. On certain ritual occasions, no stranger is allowed to enter the village. There are other days when no member of the village is permitted to leave. For the Bondas, a visit to another village is always fraught with risk. Security and peace are believed to reign only in one's own village. A man's neighbours are called *soru-bhai*, which means the brothers who have eaten the same sacrificial food. Members of other villages cannot share this privilege. The term *soru* designates a kind of food that is prepared for festivals and ritual occasions. While visitors from outside come to attend some of these events, for example wedding and funeral rituals, they are not entitled to the *soru* food.

The village is an exogamous unit. Men regard the women of their village as "mothers" or "sisters" and any kind of amorous relationship with them is strictly taboo. Men never make any indecent jokes or gestures when their women are around, even though they do so elsewhere. The Bondas say that their marriages are made between people who belong to different *sindibors* and who partake of different *soru* food, which, in short means that marriages are arranged between individuals from different villages. The girl's dormitory is open to boys of other villages, but local men are prohibited from entering.

The members of the Hill Bondas are named after the cobra and the tiger. Among the plains Bondas, there are other totemic groups: the Sun, the Monkey, the Fish and the Bear. Of the 300 marriages that were examined in the Hill Bonda genealogies by Elwin (1950), there was only

Among the Bonda, it is the women and young girls who carry wood back from the forest.
More often than elsewhere, women do more work than the men! (Jeypore region, Orissa).

one with a woman from the plains who belonged to the Bear group. All of the other marriages were between partners from the Cobra and the Tiger groups. The neighbouring tribes have more than two divisions: the Gadaba, for instance, have the Bear, the Fish, the Sun, the Monkey, the Dog, the Tortoise, the Snake and the Tiger.

These divisions are totemistic. The members of a group trace their descent from a common plant or animal ancestor. If the group is named after an animal, its members never kill or injure that animal and, indeed, revere it and seek its assistance in times of crisis. The people of their totem are their friends and treated as such. During a hunt the people of a particular totem cannot kill their totem animal and will avoid injuring it in anyway and will drop their weapons rather than cause offense to the animal. Similarly, those of the Cobra group will not kill a cobra because "it is our brother". However, among the Gadaba, if a snake enters the house of a person of the Snake fraternity, he will call a neighbour of another totemic group to kill it. He will not even remove the dead snake himself, as touching one's "ancestor" is taboo.

There is a form of ceremonial friendship made between members of the same or different villages known as *moitur* or *mahaprasad*. It is based on genuine affection and mutual support. Even when with a business purpose in mind — say, when an official is taken as a ceremonial friend — it is never broken. Ceremonial friends must lend each other firm mutual support on all occasions, and there have been instances when a feud between two villages or families has been amicably settled by people who have entered into a *moitur* friendship with one another.

A Bonda hut made of bamboo (Jeypore region, Orissa).

Bonda man preparing bamboo strips for weaving.
FOLLOWING DOUBLE PAGE: *Inside a Gadaba village.*

Making a thatched roof on the bamboo structure of a Bonda hut.
OPPOSITE PAGE: *A Bonda village on the ghats of Orissa.*

Ceremonial friends cannot marry their children to one another, are expected to offer ritual gifts when weddings take place in each other's families, and have special obligations to discharge when their ceremonial friend dies. Normally, there is some exchange of gifts whenever such friends meet. The *moitur* friendship differs from the *soru-bhai* (village brother) relationship, in that if the partners belong to different villages they cannot share the same sacred food. Once two individuals decide to enter this relationship, a ritual, supervised by a priest, is conducted, and the ceremonial friendship publicly announced.

The Bonda economy is self-sufficient. Apart from a few types of pots and cooking vessels, and some brass and bead ornaments, which they acquire from outside, they make everything they need for everyday living. They distil their own liquor and grow tobacco. In short, their dependence on the outside world is very limited.

In the past food gathering and hunting were extremely important to the Bonda. They still collect wild vegetables such as bamboo shoots and mushrooms, but hunting is practised only on festive occasions. The bow and arrows, which to this day a Bonda carries with him when going out, are now chiefly of symbolic significance and are no longer used for hunting. The massive deforestation of their hills has left hardly any wild animals to be hunted. Today, their economy is mainly dependent on agriculture, which is supplemented with pastoral produce. They rear cattle, goats and pigs, and raise poultry. As is the practice with other tribes of Orissa, they do not drink the milk of cows or goats, but eat the flesh of these animals.

Household and agricultural work is shared by both men and women but, as in other tribes, women work more and longer hours. Some observers write that men are generally seen relaxing and drinking, while their women perform all the household chores. The latter work in fields, clear the plots of land, fetch water, cook, and look after their children. When free from these tasks, they are expected to work at the loom.

An arrowhead doubles up as a needle, to stitch a Bonda shawl.
OPPOSITE PAGE: *A bead necklace being strung by a Bonda.*

Certain activities may only be performed either by men or women. Men make baskets and mats, but never weave. They must not do the husking and grinding, or the plastering of the floor with cow-dung. Fire wood must not be collected by men during the months preceding the rains, and they should not cut the hairs of adult women. Women, on the other hand, are not allowed to plough, although they can participate in all other agricultural activities. They should not climb up trees or onto the roof of a house. Sacrificial rituals may only be performed by men. Women may be diviners but not the curers of ailments. Mats are never made by them, and they never carry away a corpse or go on hunting expeditions. On ceremonial and ritual occasions, they may dance, but the beating of drums and the playing of the other musical instruments is the prerogative of men.

The Bonda practice three forms of cultivation. They carry out shifting cultivation (also known as axe cultivation and locally termed *podu*) on the steep slopes of the hills. Second, on the lowlands they cultivate cereals on terraces. They plough fields and grow dry crops like millet. Finally, they cultivate rice on irrigated and terraced fields. With population increases, and the continual felling of trees in Koraput over the centuries, it is extremely difficult for the Bonda or any other hill tribe to continue practising shifting cultivation. When Koraput was taken over by the British in 1870 as an administrative headquarters, it was already largely deforested.

Although shifting cultivation is one of the reasons for deforestation, anthropological reports do not hold tribes primarily responsible for it. The pressures on forests have multiplied over time with the permanent migration of many plains people to the hills and the reservation of certain areas by the government. Government projects are generally aimed at producing wealth that can be used for development work. The tribes thus face a situation where administrative control over their traditional sites of cultivation is being tightened, while at the same time they have to compete with migrants for rights over the hills. Unacquainted with any system of agriculture other than slash-and-burn, they have to search for other areas where they can clandestinely practice it.

Breaking the laws against shifting cultivation are severe, those caught practising it are heavily fined. More often than not, the tribes people are unable to pay the fines and end up in jail. It is clear that hill tribes prefer to move to places where they cannot easily be found using shifting cultivation rather than switching to plough cultivation. There are often fundamental beliefs at stake — the Baiga of Madhya Pradesh, for instance, believe that ploughing amounts to "tearing the breasts of Mother Earth".

In the Koraput Hills, forests are no longer available for proper shifting cultivation. The authorities have made attempts to devise some kind of controlled system that would discourage indiscriminate felling of trees. Among the Bonda, traditional shifting cultivation patterns have to a large extent been modified. Each of their households has traditional rights over the hill plots, but they are not cleared regularly as they were in the past. Only when there is a fairly substantial growth of shrubs and grasses on their plot will a family think of resorting to slash-and-burn or of selling the overgrowth to neighbours for manure. The Bondas sell their clearings to one another and mortgage them. On request, a rich person may allow his poorer relative to make use of his clearings. Sometimes, the clearings may be hired, though no rent money is paid. The owner might be presented with meat and liquor, or a share in the harvest of cucumbers and gourds.

Briefly, the process of shifting cultivation is as follows. The cutting of shrubs and grasses is ceremonially initiated by the priest in March. Apart from the mango, jackfruit, tamarind and sago palm trees, everything else is cut. The task of slashing is done by both men and women. The cleared vegetation is then heaped up and allowed to dry. The Bondas prefer to mix the grasses and shrubs that have been cut with bamboo shoots as they believe that bamboo ash yields the best manure. Once the heaps dry, they are set on fire. Any stumps of trees or large branches that remain half burnt are set on fire again until everything is reduced to ash. The ashes are then spread over the entire plot.

Young girls of the Bonda tribe.

A Gadaba woman whose enormous earrings are supported
by a cord passed over her head.

A young Bonda drinking alcohol.

The first seeds are sown after the rains. Often, fish and rice are offered to the clearings to promote soil fertility. First, different kinds of millet, all mixed together, are scattered over the earth, which is then raked with hoes. Following the planting of millet seeds, pulses of different kinds, cucumbers, and gourd and castor trees are planted. This is done by making holes in the ground with a stick, planting the seeds and then levelling the earth. When a plot is being cultivated for the first time after many years, the people are very enthusiastic and try to grow as many types of grains and vegetables as possible. Only millet is sown when the plot goes into its second year of cultivation. During the third year, the seeds are scattered without much care. The Bonda say that in the third year "the clearings produce what they like".

On the plains, the Bonda have levelled fields, which are plough cultivated. They grow crops of dry rice and black oilseed. They do not, however, grow wheat. Wet rice cultivation is carried out and they grow or gather everything else they need for their daily lives. They weave all the cloth they need and make ornaments of bark or fibre. Besides forming the staple diet of the Bonda, rice and millet are used for brewing local alcoholic drinks. They also consume fermented sap of the plan tree (*Caryota urens*). The palm trees are always owned by someone or other and are inherited along with other family possessions. They are highly prized, and there have been many disputes over their ownership. Their value derives from the importance that liquor occupies in the culture. Bonda men drink heavily and boys have their first taste of palm wine when they are being breast-fed. Elwin (1950:251) has an interesting observation to make on this: "The Bondas are addicts, in a sense that other tribesmen are not. They are not content, as the Saoras are, with their morning drink . . . They go on drinking all day." Elwin also recorded numerous cases of alcohol-induced murders.

The Bonda often build their villages among rocks. Stones are used for ordinary domestic purposes, such as erecting a wall around a field, or building a fireplace. Stone enclosures are built

Gadaba women dancing at a ceremony (Koraput region, Orissa).
OPPOSITE PAGE: *A Gadaba house decorated with paints made from natural pigments (Koraput region, Orissa).*

around young trees. But, besides being important domestically, stones are of central significance in religious rituals. The sindibor which is an identifying trait of the Hill Bonda, is a stone circle dedicated to the worship of the earth. Stones are placed on all paths to neutralise evil spirits, and gods are also symbolised by stones. Such practices prompted Furer-Haimendorf (1945) to say that the Bondas reminded him of a Megalithic culture.

For the Bonda, the supreme being is usually called Mahaprabhu, which is a Sanskrit word meaning "great lord". Elwin (1950) thinks that the use of this term in Orissa can be traced back to the founder of a Hindu devotional order. His name was Chaitanya, and in his later years he settled in Puri, a famous pilgrimage site in Orissa, where there is the celebrated temple of Lord Jagannath. Chaitanya was popularly known as Mahaprabhu, and when he reached Orissa, he was identified with Lord Jagannath himself. Later, the term Mahaprabhu came to be attached to the deity. It seems that from here the word Mahaprabhu spread to the Bonda Hills.

The cult of the Lord Jagannath is central to an understanding of both the tribal and nontribal world of Orissa. It is believed that the deity originally belonged to the Saora tribes and was later installed in the present temple by the King of Puri. In fact, the local term *mahaprasad*, used to refer to a ceremonial friend, means those who have shared the same blessed offerings (*prasada*) or food presented to Lord Jagganath. The influence of Oriya culture on the Bondas has been tremendous. They have incorporated Oriya words in their prayers and magical formulae, believing that the gods would be more pleased if their names were invoked in the language of a "superior culture".

Water is not one of the scarce commodities in the hills of Orissa. It is common to see women carrying several pots, one on top of another, on their heads.
PRECEDING DOUBLE PAGE: *View of a region inhabited by the tribes of Orissa.*

A Bonda child with his bow.
The arrowheads are generally coated with poison
prepared from plants and roots.
BELOW: *A Bonda woman working in a field.*

But what do the Bondas mean when they use the term Mahaprabhu? They certainly do not refer to Lord Jagannath. The world Mahaprabhu is of Sanskrit origin, but the Bondas have taken it to refer to the Creator who, according to them, is the sun. Often the compound term *singi-arke* (or *sih-arke*) is used to refer to the creator of the world — *singi* or *sih* meaning sun and *arke* meaning moon. It is interesting to note that the cult of the sun and the moon is found among tribes of diverse origins inhabiting different regions of India. In some communities — for example, among the Apa Tanis — there has recently been a concerted effort to revitalise such cults, which are believed to have been lost through acculturation with plains dwellers. Myths of origin of various tribes are often connected to these cults. Every tribe believes that they are the descendants of the first human beings that were created by God (or the gods).

The Bonda myth about their origin was recorded by Elwin (1950:137-38). In the beginning, it is said, there was no world. One day, Mahaprabhu spat. His spittle was eaten by a tortoise, and it conceived. The belly of the tortoise swelled but it could not deliver, and even found it impossible to move. The news of the tortoise's condition reached Mahaprabhu. He drilled a hole in the back of the tortoise and a girl was born. The girl started growing. Once she asked the tortoise who her father was, and the tortoise said that it was Mahaprabhu. She went to Mahaprabhu who refused to accept what the tortoise had told her. However, he permitted her to stay with him. Some time later, the girl caught hold of Mahaprabhu and forced him to have sex with her. The god became furious and killed her with a knife. From her blood, the earth was formed. From her right eye emerged the sun, and from the left, the moon. Her bones formed the hills. Her hair turned into all the vegetables of the world. When her belly was cut open by Mahaprabhu, a boy and a girl came out. From their cohabitation came mankind.

The myth reveals an inconsistency in Bonda belief. On the one hand, Mahaprabhu is Sun and Moon, but on the other, he is the creator of everything, including the celestial bodies. However,

Gadaba woman drinking salap *(locally brewed alcohol).*
OPPOSITE PAGE: *A Gadaba woman returns from the market carrying a coat of leaves.*
FOLLOWING DOUBLE PAGE: *The plains of Orissa during the monsoon.*

they are not troubled by this. They worship Mahaprabhu because he is kind and benevolent, but they are also aware that he can bring trouble to people if he is not placated. He must be worshipped and remembered at every turn.

The Hindu influence on Bonda thought is seen not only in their deity Mahaprabhu, but also in the way they explain the phenomenon of death. They believe that life is caused by the presence of a soul, locally called *jiwo,* which is a corrupt form of the Sanskrit word *jiva.* A person dies when Mahaprabhu sends his emissaries (*duta*) to bring the soul to the world of the sky. Like Hindus, the Bonda cremate their dead, except those who die from cholera (and in the past, smallpox) and women who die in childbirth.

The influence of Hindu thought has also penetrated the belief system of the Gadaba whose chief goddess is called Burhi Mata, Thakurani or Ganga, the goddess of smallpox and rinderpest. There is a prayer for her blessings that contains many Hindi words, but this is combined with indigenous forms of worship. For instance, pigs, goats and pigeons are sacrificed to please Thakurani. The Gadabas' funeral rituals also resemble those of their Hindu neighbours; they call the funeral feasts *pita bhoji,* which is a corrupt form of the Hindi term *pitr bhoj,* meaning "feast in honour of the ancestors". The Gadaba also have gods of land, rainfall and crops.

Finally, let us briefly glance at the Koya, a tribe inhabiting the hills in the northern part of Godavari district. The word Koya actually means "hill dweller". They are largely concentrated in the state of Andhra Pradesh, although there are small groups of them in the Jeypore Hills of Koraput district. They are very different from the Bonda and Gadaba because they are a section of the Gond tribal group of Madhya Pradesh.

The Koya are believed to have come to Orissa from Bastar district. Like the Bisonhorn Muria of Bastar district, they also sport bison-horn headdresses. They say that their ancestors left their

Gadabas at the weekly market (Orissa, near Similigurha).

original home because of famine. Their villages are small, built in groups of five or six houses, and they migrate from one place to another in search of better land.

Like the other tribes in Koraput, the Koya also practice agriculture. They grow maize, millet and cotton in their fields. Melons and gourds are grown on the roofs of their huts. They have two methods of shifting cultivation. In the first, they leave the plot of land that has been cultivated for two to three years before returning to it. In the second, the plot is left fallow for a much longer period until the trees have grown to a good height. They own large herds of cattle and goats, and engage in hunting, fishing and the collecting of minor forest produce.

The original language of the Koya used to be a branch of Gondi, but this has been lost. Those who live in Andhra Pradesh speak Telugu, while those in Orissa have adopted Oriya. Both in Andhra Pradesh and Orissa, they have lost many of their other tribal characteristics. In Andhra Pradesh, they have also lost much of their best land to outsiders, and have been reduced to the level of tenants and agricultural workers.

A Gadaba man selling fish at the market.
OPPOSITE PAGE: *Bonda carrying* salap *to the market-place.*
FOLLOWING DOUBLE PAGE: *Landscape of the ghats en route to the market (Koraput region, Orissa).*

WORSHIPPERS
OF THE FOREST SPIRITS

The hill tribes look down upon the plains dwellers, considering them inferior. If a section of a hill tribe migrates to the lowlands, relations with the rest of the tribe are automatically severed. On the plains, tribes find it difficult to retain their native customs and practices without being ridiculed by Hindus. Moreover, because of their habits and social customs, the tribes are assigned an untouchable status, and Hindus avoid having any social intercourse with them. The Binjhwars of Sambalpur district of Orissa, for example, are relegated to a low status by their Hindu neighbours because of their dietary practices. They eat pork, snake, rat and even carnivores such as panthers. Under the social conditions of the plains, such dietary and other habits are unacceptable. In other words, the members of the tribe have to de-tribalise their way of life, and this is despised by their counterparts who have remained in the hills. As we have already seen, the Bara-jangar group of the Bonda consider themselves closer to the Gadaba-Bondas than to the Bondas of the plains, because both of them live in the hills.

It is often said by hill people that the plains dwellers have absolute control over the institutions of administration, such as the revenue department, the block development office and the police, which they can always turn to their own advantage. Though they visit the plains to sell the forest produce they have collected or to buy things they themselves do not produce – like

Knife used for sacrificing animals.
OPPOSITE PAGE: *Home of the forest spirits.*

salt, kerosene oil, pots and pans, and other manufactured goods – they generally avoid interactions with the wider world.

The reason for this is that the hill tribes have always lost their land and property when dealing with outsiders, whether those living in the lowlands or those who have permanently migrated to the hills. The hill tribes, which at one time were the lords of the lands they lived on, have been gradually dispossessed of them. One of the surest methods outsiders adopted to bring this about was to advance cash loans to the tribes people. When the latter found it impossible to repay the initial sums along with the interest charged, they had to sell their lands. A 1942 report on the tribes of Jeypore Hills by Lakshimnarayan Sahu succinctly summarised this process: "Suppose you and I want to take a particular land which belongs to Kandha. Only make him indebted and try not to realise the land rent from him."

The hill tribes fear that if they move to the plains, they would be jeopardise their traditions and way of life. This fear largely accounts for their refusal to migrate to the plains even when they have been allotted cement houses by the government. On Chotanagpur Plateau (Bihar), such efforts by the government to resettle hill tribes have invariably failed. In some cases, they did move because of the fear of being prosecuted if they failed to comply, but most eventually returned to their traditional homes.

Apart from the constant fear of being exploited on the plains, the life of the hill tribes has always been inextricably bound to the forests. The forest gives them security; here they are out of reach of their enemies and obtain everything they need. The forest supplies roots, tubers and fruits that provide both food and medicines. The forest trees supply sap and flowers for the preparation of liquor. The forest is also the abode of their gods and goddesses. One of the arguments advanced by the Maler of Rajmahal Hills (Bihar) for not moving to the lowlands was that they could never leave their gods and goddesses who live in the forests. These divine powers, they say, cannot live on the plains, and the act of deserting them would make them furious. Another worry is that if their children are brought up on the plains they will refuse to obey their parents as they assimilate different values.

In other words, the hill tribes regard themselves as inseparable from the forests. All aspects of their life – whether the worship of forest spirits, or ritualised hunting, or shifting cultivation – are inextricably connected with the forests. The formulators of tribal development projects in India have realised this, and are trying to devise plans that do not require uprooting the people from their traditional habitats.

The Kandha (also written as Kond, Khond, Kondh) are a celebrated Orissan hill tribe. They are known to anthropology students for their cult of human sacrifice, which they maintained up to the mid-19th century when it was outlawed by the British government. Forming one of the largest tribes in Orissa, with a population of more than a million, they are of Dravidian stock. They mainly inhabit Koraput and Sambalpur districts and the area they live in is generally known as Kandhan or Kandhamal. Their distribution extends into central India, covering the northern parts of Kalahandi and the area south of the city of Patna, in Bihar. Because of their wide distribution in different states of India, there are regional distinctions among them, but the cult of the earth goddess is still common to all.

Little is known about the origin of the Kandha. Though they are a Dravidian people, they claim to have always been in Orissa. However, some ethnologists believe that they were driven out from the richer coastal plains of eastern India when the Aryans (the Indian branch of the Caucasian race) advanced into the region. Boal (1982:1) says, "Preferring hardship to the loss of independence, it is thought that they were forced up into the wild hill tracks of the Eastern Ghats many centuries ago." These are the areas where they still live today and in some interior villages they have been able to preserve their traditional lifestyles. There is some evidence that at one time they were rulers of the area in which they now live. It was customary until early this

A sacred and sacrificial tree in the Orissa jungle.
BELOW: *A cock being sacrificed to Mahaprabhu, the goddess Mother Earth.*
FOLLOWING DOUBLE PAGE: *Dang Bhil woman under a sacred tree (Gujarat).*

century for the oath of accession to the throne to be taken by the King of Kalahandi sitting in the lap of a Kandha. In return for the performance of these rituals on behalf of the king, they were rewarded with landed estates. The Kandha's neighbours in these hills are a "Scheduled Caste" called Pana, and others who belong to the blacksmith and potter castes. It is interesting that the latter now claim to belong to the Kandha tribe.

There is little agreement on the meaning of the world Kandha. The tribe call themselves Kuiloka or Kuienju, which may have been derived from a Telugu word, *ko* or *ku*, meaning "mountain". They also call themselves Kui. Some think that the name of another tribal group called Koya might also have derived from this term. Kui is a Dravidian language which bears in its grammatical structure a resemblance to Telugu, Tamil and Kanarese. While the Kandha speak Kui, they have also appropriated many Oriya words through their contact with Hindus in their villages and in the district towns they frequent. Another theory of the origin of their names is that it comes from the Hindi (and Sanskrit) word kandha or *skandha*, which means "shoulder". The Kandhas carry heavy loads of firewood, rice and other food grains to the village or market, and it is believed that their shoulders (*kandhas*) are very strong. It is possible that their name was given by outsiders, as often happens with tribal groups.

The Kandha Hills are a part of the Eastern Ghats and the forest cover is mixed and dense. The most prevalent and valuable tree in this region is teak (locally called *sal, Shorea robusta*). Its hard timber is used for beams in houses, and to make ploughs and other agricultural tools.

A Kandha woman lost in thought in an Orissa forest.
OPPOSITE PAGE: *A clay statue representing Mahaprabhu, the goddess Mother Earth,*
with offerings of rice, bathed in the blood of sacrificed animals.

The Kandha distil liquor from the flower of the mahua tree (*Bassia latifolia*). Their jungle yields a species of date palm and several types of grasses that provide thatching material. Wildlife abounds in the Kandha Hills. Bailey (1957) writes that this is a liability because severe damage is done to crops by wild boar, jackals, hyenas and bears. When the crops ripen, they are protected at night by the sound of beating drums or banging tins.

Although the Kandha are divided into many groups, each with its own local idiosyncrasies, they can be classed into two principal divisions: those who live in the hills and retain their traditional practices, and those who live on the plains and have absorbed certain elements of Hinduism. One of the hill-dwelling Kandha tribes is known as Kuttia Kandha; the word *kuttia* means "one who breaks or smashes". The Kuttia Kandhas are said to be so named because they kill an animal by breaking its skull. Another hill tribe is called Dongria Kandha, the word *dongria* deriving from *dongar*, which means "high-hill land". They live in the Niamgiri Hill ranges of Koraput. P.K. Nayak (1989) says that they claim their ancestry from the legendary King Niamraja.

The Kandha plains dwellers have several endogamous sub-divisions. The Raj Kandhas have landed property and enjoy the highest status. They observe the rule of endogamy very strictly. If a Raj Kandha marries a woman from another tribe he is exiled. The other important group here is called Dal Kandha. Also know as Adi Kandha, they are thought to have formerly made their living as soldiers. They have adopted Hindu customs and practices, and abstain from eating chickens and buffaloes. Like Hindus, they offer the leaves of a sacred plant *tulsi* (basil) to their deities. Those who have adopted grazing as their principal source of livelihood are called Gauria Kandha; those living in the plains of Bissaucuttack are known as Desia Kandha.

Each of the Kandha tribes is divided into totemic clans (*gossi kuda*). Their names are usually those of animals (tiger, cobra, tortoise, bear, goat, lizard and so on), plants (like pumpkin) and stones. A clan may also be named after the sun. These clans do not have the kind of dual organisation Verrier Elwin identified in the Bonda, but there is a similarity between the totems of the two tribes. The Kandha clans are exogamous, among the Dongria Kandha, often two or more may associate to form a single exogamous unit called *phratry* (*maa-kuda*).

Although divided into lineages, the unity of the clan was evident when there was a war or uprising. Thus, the clan was an important political unit, and its meetings were convened by sending messengers, who were from Pana caste, to the various Kandha settlements. At one time, each clan also had a headman, who was supposed to represent their common ancestor. The Kandha clans engaged in numerous wars and battles with neighbouring tribes as well as battling with the government.

In particular, their uprising against the government in 1837 led to great devastation. Another uprising took place in 1882 as a result of agrarian troubles. This was caused because the government had encouraged the Kolta, a skilled cultivating caste, to settle on Kandha land with the aim of developing agriculture. The Kolta soon became rich, and started advancing loans to the Kandha. When these were not repaid, they began taking possession of Kandha land. Fearing that they would soon be ousted, the Kandha clans united to attack the Kolta. The government intervened, seven of the Kandha leaders were hanged and peace was restored.

The devastation caused in Kandha territory by various conflicts and wars had serious implications for the status of clans in their society. Villagers, preferring to live peacefully, placed less value on clan unity and even less on tribe unity, instead valuing the unity of the lineage (*kutumb*). Lineages consist of family groups living in neighbouring houses within the same village. The clans, by contrast, are dispersed over a large area.

The Kandha lineages are patrilineal and exogamous. A wife may be from the same village since there is no rule of village exogamy, but the Kandha prefer to find their wives in other villages. Marriage between cousins on either the maternal or paternal side is completely prohibited. At one time wives were brought in from other tribal groups, perhaps due to the widespread

A medium of the Kandha tribe of Orissa (Nimgiri Mountains).

practice of female infanticide. However, this practice has now ended, and the Khanda have become endogamous since they no longer depend on their neighbours for wives.

The youth dormitory is an essential institution of the Kandha villages. As in other tribes of central and eastern India, one of its crucial functions is to acquaint the unmarried with sexual life. When an unmarried girl conceives, she identifies her partner, and their respective lineages arrange the marriage. Boys try to attract girls by wearing ornaments and by giving jewellery as gifts. Girls learn to play musical instruments in dormitories, and attract boys through their command of these and by singing. In some dormitories, the sleeping partners are fixed, as with the Dongria Kandha. But in all cases, the individuals know the categories of kin that must be avoided. As we saw with the Bonda, the boys never make advances towards girls of their own clan. The dormitory system is not, however, the only means of finding spouses among the Kandha; marriage also occurs through purchase, service and capture.

The Dongria Kandha have a place (called *sadar-ghar*), situated at the centre of the village, for public gatherings. This is the place where elderly men spend their leisure time and where community matters are discussed. It is constructed anew every year around the time when rituals are to be performed for the earth goddess. Musical instruments are kept here and young boys learn to play them.

The Khanda believe in the existence of 84 gods. The earth god, locally called Dharni Deota, is considered to be the supreme being. The earth goddess, known as Tari or Bera Pannu, is also

A man of the Dongria Kandha tribe on his way to the market (Nimgiri Mountains).
OPPOSITE PAGE: *Women of the Dongria Kandha tribe trekking through the jungles of Orissa, on their way to Muniguda market.*

Dongria women on their way to Muniguda market.
BELOW: *A Gadaba woman.*

very important. The Khanda also believe in the existence of a large number of spirits who are often represented as stones. Of principal importance to them are three festivals closely connected with their agricultural calendar, which are respectively celebrated in March, September and November. In each the earth god is worshipped by sacrificing a goat or chicken.

Once the most important ritual among the Kandha was the worship of the earth goddess. Human sacrifice was made to gain her favour. Locally called *meriah* sacrifice, a detailed account of this ritual were provided by Major William Macpherson and Major-General John Campbell, the two officers employed to suppress human sacrifice in Orissa. According to their reports, which were compiled by James Frazer in his celebrated book *The Golden Bough*, the term *meriah* referred to the victim sacrificed to the earth goddess.

This sacrifice aimed at ensuring good crops, especially turmeric. The Kandha belief was built on it. Their goddess accepted the victim who the Kandha had purchased by selling some of their children. The victim, being a consecrated person, was treated with deference and fed well before being sacrificed. The Kandha believed that the fertility of the soil, and the chances of achieving a general state of well-being could be increased if they could obtain some part of the body of the sacrificial victim. After the sacrifice, the tribes people struggled to get a piece of his flesh, drops of his blood, spittle or tears. The remains of his flesh were rolled in leaves and buried in the cultivated fields. With his blood, spittle and tears, the worshippers anointed their heads. It was believed that the blood would dye the turmeric and the tears would bring rain. The last human

Dongria Kandhas carrying Pandanus leaves
which are used as plates (Nimgiri Mountains).

A Dongria tribeswoman at Muniguda market (Orissa).
OPPOSITE PAGE: *Kandha woman selling tobacco
at Muniguda market (Orissa).*

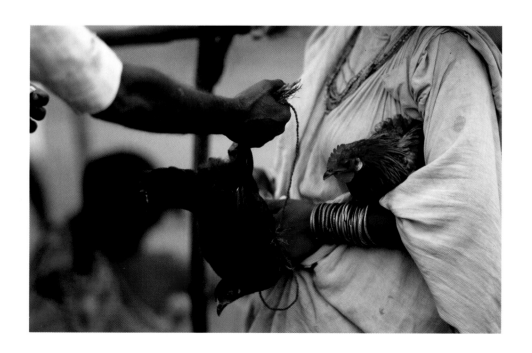

A tiled house of the Kuttia Kandha (Orissa).

These tree trunks in a Cheriaka Kandha village were once used as platforms for human sacrifice.
Today animals are sacrificed instead.

The veranda of a low-roofed Kandha house (Orissa).
OPPOSITE PAGE: A Kandha village (Orissa).
BELOW: A Dang Bhil baby in her cradle (Gujarat).

sacrifice in Kandha land occurred in 1852, though there is evidence that the King of Jeypore sacrificed a 13–year–old girl to the goddess Durga after succeeding to the throne in 1860-1. Forty years later, the Kandhas substituted a buffalo for a human being as a sacrificial offering.

The Kandha were unique, other Orissan hill tribes did sacrifice non-totemistic animals to their deities, but never humans. There was, however, one case of human sacrifice in the Chattisgarh region of Madhya Pradesh, where Thakur Deo, a local god, was placated in this manner.

The divinities of hills and forests are shared by many tribal groups. Along with these common deities, there are others that are exclusive to a particular tribe. For instance, the Paraja of Orissa have Danteswari as an important goddess in their religious system. Danteswari is primarily worshipped in the Bastar district of Madhya Pradesh. Her worship survives among the Paraja because they are believed to have originally come from Bastar. Their other customs, dress and ornaments are reminiscent of the Gond of Madhya Pradesh, particularly the tattooing of the breasts and arms of their women.

Let us conclude this chapter with a brief look at the southern Indian hill tribes. Most of them still practice food gathering and hunting, and are finding it difficult to adjust to a changing world. They have been worst affected by deforestation and in some cases their population has been declining. The tribes of the Andaman Islands are a good example of this. Among the other food gathering and hunting tribes are the Allar, Chingathar, Kadar, Korager, Kurumbar, Mala Malasar, Mudugar and Sholagar.

The Kadar, who number about 2,000, are well-known in the ethnological literature of India because of their woolly hair type, which reminds one of African Negros. B.S. Guha regarded them as the original inhabitants of India. Their settlements consist of neatly constructed huts made of bamboo and are thatched with leaves from teak and bamboo trees. Special huts exist for women for use during menstruation and childbirth.

At one time, the Kadar were nomads. But once the British government declared that the right to collect minor forest produce belonged exclusively to the hill tribes, some of the Kadar started working for the government-appointed contractors in their region. They collected wax, honey, cardamom, ginger, turmeric, elephant tusks and so on, and worked in the forest department. The others, however, remained food-gatherers. Currently there are three groups within the tribe; those who are still food-gatherers and hunters; those working with contractors who exploit minor forest produce; and those who have now settled down to become cultivators.

The Kadar used to practice polygyny. Each wife had her own hearth and cooking utensils, the first wife enjoying precedence over the others. Today they are monogamous. Their myth of origin involves two hill gods who were brother and sister. Emerging from the netherworld, they were the first to inhabit the earth and from their incestuous union came the first of the Kadar men and women.

The Kadar bury their dead, and two years after a death a memorial feast is held in the deceased's honour. The dead are believed to go to heaven which, according to local belief, is in the sky. But they always keep an eye on this world, and so are propitiated because they are thought to provide food and game, and protect the living against fierce wild animals. Before any honey collection or hunting expedition the Kadar make offerings to them.

The Mala Malasar (also called Malayar), like the Kadar, are collectors of forest produce though they also work as agricultural labourers. They used to live in Kerala, but now large numbers have moved to Coimbatore district (Tamil Nadu). There are two main groups within the tribe, which are racially distinct: the Nattu Malasar, who are matrilineal, and the Kongu Malasar, who are patrilineal.

The huts of the Mala Malasar are constructed from bamboo. Sometimes they build them on tree tops as a precaution against wild animals. The cult of the sun and the moon has an important place in their ritual system and it is customary for them to bow before the rising sun.

In a Mala Malasar village a woman grinds grain into flour (Kerala).

Mala Malasar children (Kerala).

As we pointed out earlier, however, the influence of Hinduism on the religious systems of tribes has increased over the last century. This is no less true of the tribal groups of southern India and we can expect to see groups like the Kadar and Mala Malasar modify their beliefs and practices still further in the years to come.

A man of the Kandha tribe (Orissa).
OPPOSITE PAGE: *A Kadar tribeswoman with her child (Kerala).*

WATER TRACKS

"Water is the elixir (*amrit*) of life. It is the most precious wealth of mankind. Its value is realised when one is deprived of it." So said a Bhil tribesman of the great Thar Desert.

Towns and villages have usually grown up around rivers and lakes, and when they have dried up, or the river has changed its course, or there has been a fall in the water-table people have moved to new locations. The Indus Valley Civilisations (3,500 BC), which developed in areas presently in India and Pakistan, is a good example of the importance of water sources. One of the most probable explanations for its decline, according to paleo-climatologists, is that the River Saraswati, which supported the civilisations, gradually dried up and forced the people to move to other areas.

The District Gazetteers of western Rajasthan and Kutch list several uninhabited villages. They were all depopulated because the wells that supplied them with water dried up. Studies have shown that the Thar Desert is advancing towards the Indo-Gangetic plain, and in the future the lack of water will become increasingly acute in the areas bordering the desert. Even today, most of the villages on the borders of the desert are dependent on water tankers provided by the state government. Such scarcity makes people use water frugally. For example, it is common to see people in the villages of Rajasthan washing their hands or feet near a tree so that the "used water" is not "wasted"; they say that "what is not useful to us is of considerable use to other

A fishing boat on Chilka Lake (Orissa).
OPPOSITE PAGE: *A fisherman on the Brahmaputra River at Guwahati (Assam).*

Fisherman on the Brahmaputra (Assam).
PREVIOUS DOUBLE PAGE: *Fishermen on the Brahmaputra (Assam).*

living beings". Water is preserved in tanks built underneath the compound of a house. Called *kothis*, they are very deep for two reasons – to collect as much water as possible and to guard against evaporation. Whenever needed, water is lifted with a bucket. Where there is such scarcity, frequent bathing or washing of clothes, animals or the compound of the house become unrealistic. People do not feel unclean in their mud-impregnated clothes, or when they have to go without a bath for weeks or even months. There are villages in Rajasthan and Kutch that are still today dependent on rain-fed ponds: the animals are bathed and clothes are washed in them, and during the summer children swim in them. They are also the only sources of drinking water, and so are contaminated and unsafe. Health department reports frequently point out that stomach infections, including cholera, are endemic.

There are other parts of India where water is available in abundance and rainfall is very heavy. Here tribes people adopt very different methods for coping with their environment. The tribes living near the Brahmaputra, the great river of Assam, have built a variety of canoes to cross the river. Sometimes, the canoes are attached to rafts on both sides to prevent them from being capsized. Fishing is one of the most common economic activities. People go out to fish in streams and rivers, and they also create fish-ponds in their fields, as they do in northeast India. Wet rice cultivation is possible in areas of high rainfall, and in eastern and southern India, where rainfall is adequate, rice is the staple diet of the people, in contrast to the north where wheat has precedence over rice.

Houseboats on the Brahmaputra (Assam).

Legal ownership of water is crucial to both peasant and tribal India, though big rivers are regarded as common property. Until untouchability was legally abolished in India, upper-caste people did not allow untouchables to bathe in, or draw water from, rivers because they regarded them as sacred. Although the law has changed, the contemporary practice of untouchability often continues to revolve around access to water sources. The higher castes insist that untouchables should either have their own separate wells or fetch water from streams where there is no caste monopoly.

One tribe's attitude toward the ownership of water illustrates its significance. The Angami Nagas, Hutton (1969) writes, regard water as a "very valuable property". Rights are acquired over water; for example, the man who first digs a channel to tap a new stream, thereby obtains a right to the water drawn; this stream cannot then be tapped higher up (though it can be tapped downstream). The channel and the water that is drawn from it become the subject of rights that can be inherited or purchased. In lowland villages, wells and ponds are owned by both individuals and castes. A well dug in someone's cultivated field is his property, and can only be used with his permission. The authorities often receive complaints about the illegal use of water, especially during the agricultural season.

Water has become an important symbol in many cultures. The best known of these are the concepts of holy water and holy rivers, the latter being generally personified as female. The Ganges, for instance, is regarded as a Hindu goddess, which flows from the tresses of Lord

A tribesman washing his buffalo (Andhra Pradesh).

Shiva. Many Hindus believe that some drops of holy water from the Ganges should be poured into the mouth of a dying person.

There are similar beliefs among the tribal societies of India. The Sema Naga, for example, conceive of every river as a living being. One of their rivers, called Dayang, plays a role in their system of dispute settlement. Like the other Naga tribes, they resolve their disputes by both parties taking an oath before one of their deities. It is believed that whoever swears falsely will be punished by the spirits, and that symptoms of supernatural wrath, such as illness or death, will affect the person involved directly or members of his family. Such symptoms are regarded as providing sufficient evidence for the village elders to make a judgement against him. Furthermore, the Sema believe that the supernatural powers will keep on punishing someone who falsely swears an oath for the rest of his life. Among the Sema, the most serious oath is the one taken before the Dayang River. Whoever swears falsely there, the Sema say, will never be able to drink its water or eat its fish.

Tribal societies also have myths regarding the origin of rivers and water. In some of these, the creators of human beings also created the rivers. The Ao Naga say, according to Mills (1973), that water was first shown to a group of tribes people (called "water-finders") by a bulbul bird. A similar myth is held by some of the Manipuri tribes. The water of one's original settlement is regarded as the purest and the most sacred; thus when the Lhota Nagas move to a new settlement, they always bring with them water from a spring in their old village. This is then poured

Fisherman of the Muria tribe catching small fish
in a rice field during the monsoon season (Madhya Pradesh).

Fishermen of the Moduval tribe (Perambikulam region, Kerala).
BELOW: *Muria fisherman (Madhya Pradesh).*

into the water sources of their new settlement, and they say that in this way the original source continues to sustain them. To deal with the scarcity of water, both tribal and peasant societies in India depend largely on their religion and magic. In Rajasthan and Gujarat there are water diviners who will be consulted to determine whether a particular piece of land has enough underground water or where a well should be dug. The scientific opinion of a geologist about the presence or absence of water is invariably confirmed by consulting one of these diviners. When it does not rain for a long time, the people worship their deities, make offerings to the god of fire (*yajna*), and sometimes sacrifice animals. Among the Kandha, as we saw, one of the aims of human sacrifice was to ensure plentiful rain in future years. In Manipur it was thought that the blood of captives could bring rain. Although there is no evidence of human sacrifice being made for this purpose, it is known that ponies were frequently sacrificed.

Some tribes do not have a specific rain-making (or "rain-compelling") ritual; they propitiate their deities in the usual way, requesting them to "send" rain. However, there are others who have a specific set of rain-making rituals, and some of them also have rain-making specialists. In some of these rituals, the people simulate the conditions associated with rain. Sir James Frazer called this imitative or mimetic magic in his celebrated book *The Golden Bough*. One example of this comes from the Munda of Bihar who, in the early morning of the chosen day for performing the rain-making magic, climb up the nearest hill and push down all the stones they can find. Some other tribesmen stand at the foot of the hill and, as the stones roll down, being beating

A Muria cattle herd in a monsoon shower (Madhya Pradesh).

drums. The rumbling noise of the falling stones is intensified by the drum beat, and the Munda believe that this produces thunder which will be followed by rain.

The rain-compelling ceremony of the Meitie of Manipur described by T.C. Hodson (1908) is another good example of imitative magic. The Meitie performed this ceremony on a hill situated to the east of Imphal, the capital of Manipur. On its upper slopes, there was a stone that resembled an umbrella. The King of Manipur, who was supposed to perform rituals on behalf of his people, carried up water from a deep spring at the bottom of the hill and sprinkled it on the "umbrella stone". This ceremony symbolised the hope that even the deepest springs would be full in future. Similarly, the Ao Naga performed the rain-making ceremony wearing rain-shields over their heads as if it was raining. And among the Lhota Naga, a rattling noise was made to imitate the sound of falling rain.

Some tribes also practice rain-stopping rituals. The Birhor of Bihar, who are mainly food gatherers, dislike heavy rain because it interferes with their daily routine. The youngest member of a family places mahua flowers (*Bassia latifolia*) into an earthen jug that is then filled with water. The mouth of the jug is covered with a leaf and a string tied around it. The pot is then lowered into a hole dug in the ground, and the earth is levelled. The Birhor say that by performing this ritual they "bury" the rain for some time. Other tribes also claim knowledge of rain-stopping rituals, but prefer not to practise them for fear of dire consequences. The Angami Naga know a rain-stopping ritual, but they say that if it is practised, the rain would stop for seven years.

Forest around Chitrakoot during the monsoon (Madhya Pradesh).
FOLLOWING DOUBLE PAGE: *Bhil women washing their saris (Gujarat).*

Bhil women bathing in the river.

Hill Saora villager washing his bullocks (Orissa).
BELOW: *Koya children gathering water-lilies (Orissa).*

FOLLOWING DOUBLE PAGE: *Dang Bhil tribeswomen working in rice fields in the forest (Gujarat).*

The bamboo hats of the hill Saora women (Orissa).
PRECEDING DOUBLE PAGE: *These Dang Bhil women have put aside their leaf raincoats while they work (Gujarat).*
OPPOSITE PAGE: *A Gond woman returning from the fields with her child (Orissa).*
PAGE 102-103: *Working in the rice fields during the monsoon (Madhya Pradesh).*
PAGE 104-105: *Working in the rice fields (Andhra Pradesh).*

WANDERERS

The absence of vegetation in the desert regions of western India, caused by a lack of water and low soil fertility, forces the people who live in them to lead nomadic or semi-nomadic lives. The harshness of the environment, which no development project, however ambitious or well-funded, can counter, means that there is also a very low population density. In Kutch, for example, there are only 19 people per square kilometre compared with 136 per square kilometre in the state of Gujarat as a whole.

However, the thorny vegetation of the western desert supports a large number of sheep and camels. According to the 1972 livestock census, India was home to 39.31 million sheep in that year, of which 8.5 million were in Rajasthan. Of the 1.1 million camels in 1985, more than 70 per cent were in Rajasthan. Sheep can subsist, and often flourish, on a coarse diet which other domestic animals will not accept. Most of the world's sheep are raised in dry, stony, or mountainous regions that are generally unfit for agricultural purposes. Camels are equally well adapted to barren lands.

As the vegetation in the arid and semi-arid parts of western India is sparse, the tribes who rear animals such as sheep and camels have to lead nomadic lives. In Kutch, it is estimated that on average, 5,000 families migrate each year in search of grazing grounds, taking along with

Women and children of the Rabari tribe (Kutch, Gujarat).
OPPOSITE PAGE: *An old man of the Rabari tribe, resting in front of his house (Kutch, Gujarat).*

them as many as 700,000 sheep and goats, 40,000 cows and oxen, and perhaps 2,000 camels and donkeys. The groups involved in livestock production can be conveniently divided into two categories:

Those for whom livestock production is their principal occupation. These include the Rabari and the Sindhi Muslims of western Rajasthan; the Rabari of Kutch, Jamnagar and Kathiawar (Gujarat); the Bharwad of Gujarat; the Gaddi of Himachal Pradesh; the Gujar of Kashmir and Garhwal; and several shepherd castes of the Deccan Plain and southern India;

Those who are predominantly engaged in agricultural activities but for whom pastoralism is nevertheless a significant element of their economy. These include the Bhatti Rajputs of Jaisalmer; the Bishnoi of Rajasthan; and the Jats, Rajputs and Ahir in other parts of India.

Besides these groups, the arid west of India also has non-pastoral nomad communities, such as the Gadulia Lohar. Another very important tribal group, the Bhil, combines agriculture and pastoralism with hunting. In the following pages we will look at the lives of some of these communities.

The Bishnoi are an outstanding example of the transformation of a sect into a caste. Mostly found in Rajasthan, they are the worshippers of Vishnu, who is, according to Hindu mythology, the "god who nurtures". Their sect was founded by a Panwar Rajput called Jambhaji (also called Jambheswarji Maharaja), who was born in a village in Bikaner in 1451 and spent his early life grazing his father's cattle. It is said that Jambhaji remained completely silent until he reached the age of 34. A Brahmin was sent by his parents to make him speak but failed. Once the Brahmin admitted defeat, however, Jambhaji manifested his power by lighting a lamp with a snap of his

Extracting salt from the swamps in the Gulf of Kutch, Gujarat.
FOLLOWING DOUBLE PAGE: *A plain inundated by the sea, near Anjar in the Gulf of Kutch.*
PAGE 112-113: *Maldharis in the saline plains of Kutch.*

fingers. He then uttered his first word. Following this momentous event, he left his home to live on a sand hill. During the great famine of 1485, Jambhaji is said to have provided food to all those who expressed faith in his preaching, and in this way he gained a large following.

His sayings, collected by his disciples, number 120 and his followers are enjoined to strictly observe 29 of these. Some say that the term Bhisnoi is made up of two words, *bis* meaning 20 and *no*(w) meaning nine, to constantly remind people of the 29 central principles. However, it seems to us that these people call themselves Bishnoi because they worship Vishnu, and believe that the founder of their sect is his incarnation. The 120 principles deal with both prescribed and prohibited behaviour. For example, it is good to bathe in the morning, to be careful in one's speech and to wear clothes that are blue in colour; but one should not kill animals, or cut down green trees, or plough with bullocks.

Some of these precepts, like wearing blue, are not strictly followed. Indeed, elders of the Bishnoi sect prefer to wear white clothes. And when ploughing the land, they do use pairs of bullocks, though, as is common in Rajasthan, camels are also used. Some of the precepts are however very strictly followed. Bishnois are widely admired in India for the respect they show to both trees and animals, and it is believed that the well-known Chipko Movement in the Himalayas to save trees from being felled by "hugging" them had its origins in Rajasthan. An old story supports this theory. An 18th-century king of Jodhpur state (in Rajasthan) wanted to build a palace. To collect the wood needed for its construction, the king's axe-men arrived in a

Bishnoi village (Thar Desert, Rajasthan).
OPPOSITE PAGE: *It is common for Rabari tribeswomen to dress in black (Kutch, Gujarat).*

Rabari child (Anjar region).
BELOW AND OPPOSITE PAGE: *Young woman of the Motwa tribe,*
in the village of Banni (Rann of Kutch).

Bishnoi village known as Jalnadi that had big trees, locally called *khejri*. As they declared their intention to fell the trees and announced that this was by royal command, a Bishnoi woman ran forward and begged them not to go ahead. She told them that the community would not allow them to cut even one branch, and if they remained adamant the village women (the men were away working in the fields at the time) would give their lives to save the trees. The woman's pleas were ignored and the royal contractor ordered his men to proceed with their task. The Bishnoi woman ran to one of the trees and put her arms around it. The contractor could not persuade her to leave and finally ordered his men to axe her and the tree down. As she fell, other women from all the nearby villages came forward to evict the contractor and his men, and save the trees from being cut down. It is said that 359 women and men from 49 Bishnoi villages gave their lives that day to save the trees. Every year a fair is organised to commemorate the great sacrifice of the Bishnoi, it is called Khajarla after the tree that was saved.

The Bishnoi's attitude towards animals is also characterised by compassion. Their villages are often overrun by antelopes and other animals but they are never harmed. They also say that merit (*punya*) can be earned by scattering grain for birds, and by releasing caged birds. In those villages where the Bishnoi predominate, they do not allow any of the other castes to consume non-vegetarian food. This campaign against meat eating in Rajasthan has been strengthened by the support of the Jain sect; like the Bishnoi, wherever they have numerical and political dominance, they have been successful in upholding vegetarian ideals.

Rabaris taking a break from work.

As the Bishnoi are a sect, membership of their group has been open to different castes. William Crooke has observed that although the sect has been theoretically open to all, in practice only members of the clean (i.e., non-untouchable) castes have joined it. These castes have continued to be endogamous in spite of their new common identity, so there are now several different Bishnoi castes – the Jat Bishnoi, Bania Bishnoi and Ahir Bishnoi. In recent years, however, attempts have been made to foster a greater unity among them, not by dissolving the internal caste system, but by the community building rest-houses, schools, dispensaries, veterinary hospitals, and so on.

The Bishnoi are a prosperous community, and the level of education among them is high when compared to many other groups. Some of the senior bureaucratic, professional and political positions in Rajasthan and neighbouring states are occupied by them, and one of the chief ministers of the state of Haryana was a Bishnoi.

The Bishnoi do not employ members of the Hindu priestly caste (Brahmins) to carry out their rituals, they are conducted by their own priests, or Sadh. The Bishnoi recite the sayings of their founder Jambhaji and read those Hindu texts that revolve around Lord Vishnu. As cutting down trees is prohibited, they do not burn their dead on wooden pyres as is the practice among Hindus. Earlier they used to bury their dead in the courtyard of the house, but now they immerse the corpse in rivers or streams, attached to sandbags to weigh them down.

A young Maladhari woman from Bandiajara village in the Gulf of Kutch (Gujarat).
OPPOSITE PAGE: *A Rabari village on the saline plains in the south of Kutch.*
PAGE 122: *Young girl of the Rabari tribe dressed in silver jewellery (Anjar).*
PAGE 123: *Young Rabari woman wearing a blouse decorated with mirrors (Mindiyana village in Kutch).*

The Bhil are very different to the Bishnoi. They have earned a reputation as excellent hunters. Indeed, the name Bhil is said to be derived from the Dravidian word for bow. Till recently, this used to be their preferred weapon and like the Naga who never stepped out of their houses without a *dao* (sword), Bhil men were always seen with a bow and arrow slung over their shoulders.

The Bhil are one of India's largest tribal groups, their present population being estimated at around five million. Their origin is a mystery. Earlier ethnologists believed that their original dialect, which they simply called Bhili, was not of the Indo-Aryan family of languages. However, this language is not used any longer as the Bhil have adopted the language of whichever area they have lived in. There is some variation in the lifestyles of the different Bhil groups who are spread out over western Madhya Pradesh, Rajasthan, eastern Gujarat and northern Maharashtra. It is quite possible that the name of their tribe is not their own, but was given to them by the Hindus.

The Bhil figure prominently in Hindu mythology and classical texts. There is a story about them in the *Mahabharata*, the famous Hindu epic. Once, there was a great teacher of archery called Dronacharya. He used to train the princes (who belonged to the *kshatriya* or warrior caste) in this art. A Bhil king's son called Eklavya approached him for training, but Dronacharya refused to take him as his pupil. Eklavya, steadfast in his determination, made a clay idol of Dronacharya and, bowing before it everyday, practised archery. One day, Dronacharya and his pupils happened to pass the spot where Eklavya was practising. Dronacharya asked who his

This Jath Hotwa tribeswoman is wearing a nose ring. It indicates that she is married (Hodka, Kutch).
OPPOSITE PAGE: *A young Rabari boy in his festive clothes (Mindiyana village in Kutch).*

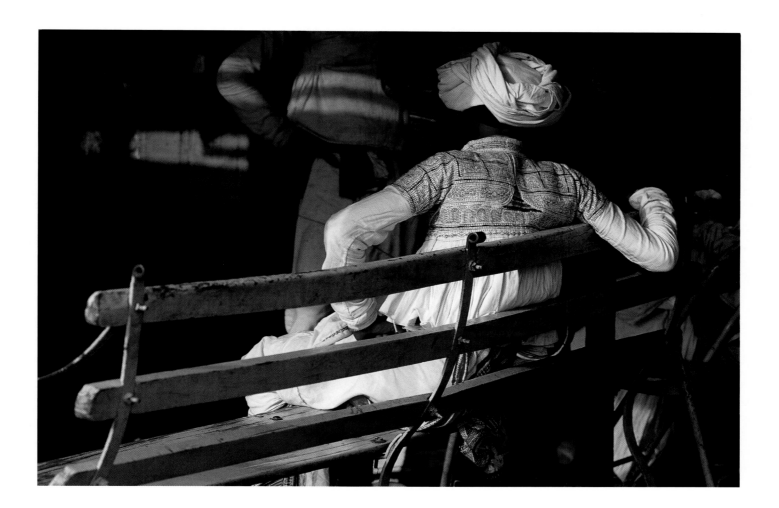

teacher was, and on hearing his own name invited Eklavya to compete against his pupils. One by one, each of the princes who had been trained by Dronacharya lost. The last one to compete was Arjuna, the hero of the *Mahabharata*. Dronacharya did not want anyone to be better than Arjuna at archery, so he demanded a fee (*gurudakshina*) from Eklavya for having learned archery from his clay image. The fee Dronacharya asked for was Eklavya's right thumb (which was crucial for his archery). Without hesitation, Eklavya offered his thumb. From that day on, Bhil abandoned the use of the thumb when shooting arrows, using their fore and middle fingers instead.

Until the 19th century, the Bhil practised shifting cultivation. The British abolished this way of life and helped them to adapt to settled agriculture. They have now completely taken to plough cultivation, but the hilly sites they own have poor soil and the yield is low. To supplement their income the Bhil usually work as agricultural labourers. They also collect and sell jungle produce, and like the Grasia of Rajasthan, sell firewood.

The *kshatriya*, or warrior caste, of Rajasthan still recognises the Bhil as the original inhabitants of the area. In some of the princely states, it was customary for a ruler to receive a mark (*tilak*) on his forehead from a Bhil, which the Bhil made with blood from an incision in his right thumb. Similar customs are found in other tribes, and invariably indicate a special relationship between them and their rulers. They have had implications for the tribes' status; sometimes, they received land grants and in others they were given a place in the local caste hierarchy thereby transforming a "tribe" into a "caste".

The Jats are a good example of a tribe becoming a caste. The term Jat has been used for a multitude of groups with different cultural and ethnic backgrounds living in parts of northern India and Pakistan. Today they are a caste like any other; they are fervent Hindus, and in almost all parts of northern India they are big landowners.

A Rabari shepherd in Anjar (Kutch, Gujarat).
OPPOSITE PAGE: *Interior of a Rabari hut. This piece of clay furniture has been decorated with mirror inlay by women during Diwali, the festival of lights (Kutch).*

In Kutch, however, all Jats are Muslims. Their oral tradition testifies that they were originally pastoralists who lived in an area called Halaf, situated between the border separating Iran and Iraq. Several centuries ago, they left their homeland in search of fertile grazing grounds and, passing through Sindh, they settled in Kutch. In Kutch, some of them, now known as the Gracia Jats, adopted agriculture. Others became holy men, devoting themselves to the study of religious texts, and became known as the Fakirani Jats. A third group, called the Dhanetah Jats, remained herdsmen. All three groups recognise a common ancestry and frequently intermarry.

The Rabari, who breed and herd camels, are an outstanding example of a community that assumes different social identities in different areas. They are chiefly concentrated in the states of Gujarat and Rajasthan. In Gujarat they are regarded as a "Scheduled Tribe" and are therefore entitled to all the privileges resulting from the government's policy on Schedule Tribes. But in Rajasthan (where the Rabari are also called Raika and Devasi), they are denied the status of tribe and are instead listed as an "Other Backward Class" or a "Semi-Nomadic Community". Whatever the official classification, in both these states they consider themselves to be a caste (*jati*).

Numbering more than 400,000, the Rabari are also found in villages in Haryana, Punjab and Uttar Pradesh. Their myth of origin provides insights into the way they see themselves. According to the Rabari, Lord Shiva, the Hindu god of creation and destruction, was in deep meditation for 12 years. His consort, Parvati, occupied herself with various playful activities.

During a public ceremony at the temple, a Rabari child receives the name that the gods have chosen for him.
OPPOSITE PAGE: *Young Bhil woman of Rajasthan.*
FOLLOWING DOUBLE PAGE: *Plains in southern Kutch near Anjar during the monsoon season.*

Using clay, she made objects using the shapes of various bodily parts. When Shiva emerged from his meditation, she asked him to infuse life into the objects. One by one, each object was transformed and came to life, and that is how the animal world was created. Finally, there came the turn of an object that had five legs, the fifth one being stuck to its belly. Shiva pointed out the grave difficulty such an animal would have in walking, but at Parvati's insistence, he said, "*utha*", meaning "get up". From that day, the animal came to be known as an untha, or camel. But as expected, it had difficulties in moving, so Shiva pushed the fifth leg upwards, and it emerged as a hump. As soon as the camel had four legs, it started running swiftly and often disappeared into the wilderness. Shiva decided to create a man who could look after the animal. From the "dirt" of his skin, he created a grazier who he named Chamar (meaning "leather"). Since he had emerged from the divine body, he was also called Devasi, "he in whom dwells the god". Shiva then decided to arrange a marriage for Chamar. He advised him to go to the river and bring back the clothes of the celestial nymphs who came to bathe there regularly. Chamar collected the clothes of a nymph called Gavri and took them to Shiva. The nymph followed him as Shiva had planned and the two were subsequently married with the god's blessing. Their progeny became known as Rabari.

To sanctify the marriage, Shiva proclaimed ten commandments. These include Monday is the "day" of Lord Shiva which should be observed as a day of fasting and on such days mourning rituals should be avoided; every family should maintain a herd of camels, and wherever the herd

Young Rabari boy on the day of his baptism, which takes place at a sacred place.
OPPOSITE PAGE: *Seminomadic Rabaris gather for the annual ceremony of collective baptism.*

stopped to rest install a flag of ochre colour; the aak plant (*Calotropis procera*) is the abode of Lord Shiva and should not therefore be used as fuel.

This myth explains why the Rabari are camel breeders. Even now, when camel herds are considered less useful and are largely disappearing in Rajasthan, every Rabari household tries to keep at least one camel in his herd. The belief that the caste came into being with Chamar's theft of the nymph's garments explains why clothing has a special significance to the Rabari.

Why are these people called Rabari? Crooke (1896:201) believed that the term was derived for *rahwar*, meaning "quick-paced, active". One explanation for this is that in some states the Rabari were employed to distribute the inter-state mail (*dak*) and they were generally seen as "camel-riding messengers". Another explanation is that in certain princely states in Gujarat, such as Porbandar, Rabari were frequently employed as soldiers, an occupation which, no less than carrying the mail, required swiftness of foot. Crooke does not tell us the language from which this word is derived. However, Westphal-Hellbusch (1975:125) says that the word Rabari consists of two words, *raha* meaning "outside" and *bari* meaning "way" The combination effectively means, "people who are outside the established way". The Rabari of Gujarat believe that they acquired their name because of the marriage of their ancestor with a nymph, which was "outside" the normal principle of caste endogamy.

The Rabari are not native to the region they now inhabit. In all probability their ancestors were from Iran and migrated to India, via the north-west frontier, in search of new breeding

A young Rabari boy at the temple.

grounds for their herds. Sherring (1879:246) in the second volume of *Hindu Castes and Tribes* writes that "most of them have the peculiar Persian physiognomy. One of their family names is Aga, which seems to support their Persian descent."

In one of the earliest studies of the Rabari of Gujarat, Mankad (1939:31-2) says that they used to live in Baluchistan. As the country was mountainous, sandy and barren, they started domesticating dromedaries, which they trained for long journeys. The animals' milk was used to prepare clarified butter (*ghee*) and its hair was used to make coarse cloth. As their population increased, they started moving out to other areas. Through the north-west, they entered Rajasthan, and from there, they came to Kutch.

In Rajasthan, the Rabari invariably live outside the main village in separate hamlets called *dhani*. This is not because their caste status is defiling, as with the untouchable castes, but because they have always needed to live close to their grazing grounds. A dhani is usually a kin-based group comprising all those who claim a common descent. However, in a big hamlet, two or more such descent lines may coexist. The Rabari say that they can take up residence in any Rabari hamlet simply by announcing their identity, and anyone denying them the privilege is liable to be fined by their case council.

The Rabari are Hindus. Since they believe that they have descended from Lord Shiva, he is their supreme deity. They also worship a goddess known as Mammai, an angry form of Shiva's consort. It is believed that she once asked her husband to refrain from meditation, but he

A Rabari child at the doorway of her house.

ignored her request. From that day on she resolved to remain mute, and her priests (*moga*) do not speak when engaged in rituals.

Pabuji, who is credited with having given the camel to the tribe, is another deity of the Rabari. Every Raika hamlet has a temple or stone platform dedicated to Pabuji that is looked after by a local elder. On every auspicious occasion in the family, an offering of sugar wafer (*batasha*) and coconut is made to him. When a camel is sick, the Rabari vow to make an offering to Pabuji once the animal recovers.

As with the Jats, the Rabari have absorbed the characteristics of the region they inhabit. In certain parts of Gujarat, for example, they domesticate cows and buffaloes. Once, they regarded sheep and goat breeding as inferior to camel breeding. But with changing times, they have all taken to rearing flocks of sheep and goats. When there is inadequate vegetation in their area they move with their animals to other areas for eight to nine months of the year.

The pastoralists life is extremely difficult in the arid zones of both Rajasthan and Gujarat. The increasing use of land for agricultural purposes has led to a shrinkage in the available pasture land and this has hit them hard. As irrigation facilities are largely non-existent in most of the desert areas, agriculture is basically rain fed and most of the villages depend on a single crop. Some of the crops harvested are generally stored for future use as the threat of drought is ever possible if the crop is bountiful, the peasant thinks of selling off his surplus. Given the harsh conditions of the arid areas of Rajasthan and Gujarat, it is incredible that they have produced some of the most colourful clothes and intricate jewellery to be seen in India. We shall take a look at these later.

Rabari shepherds gather around the temples with their priest,
who acts as the gods interpreter, for the 'name giving' ceremony.

THE WARRIORS
WITH
LONGHOUSES

M any radically different racial and ethnic groups inhabit northeast India. Within a relatively small area there co-exists different ideologies and mutually incomprehensible languages. The geographical character of the area also varies considerably. The Brahmaputra Valley is broad and almost level. It is surrounded by rugged highlands covered by tropical forests.

The diversity of this region is exaggerated by the fact that the Mongoloid groups of the hills are part of Southeast Asian culture while the lowland populations belong to South Asian culture. Ideological variations reflect these patterns. The followers of Mahayana Buddhism live mostly in the hill regions; the lowland populations are primarily Hindu. In recent times, however, the Christian missions have been very active in the hills, and have succeeded in converting the indigenous tribes to their faith. Comprising seven states, popularly known as "seven sisters", Northeast India is home to several well-known tribal groups. Some of these states are in fact called "tribal states" by the Government of India. Among the groups who live there, some, like the Naga and the Mizo, have played an important role in the history of tribal struggle in India. However, relatively little is known about most of other tribes of this region. The tribes living within the state boundary of Arunachal Pradesh are the least well known. Most of them have been able to preserve their customs and way of life up to the present day, because of their isolation from the mainstream of Indian society.

A Nishi longhouse.
OPPOSITE PAGE: *Nishi warrior (Arunachal Pradesh).*

The hills of the northeast region remained completely isolated until the British moved into Upper Assam to develop the tea industry in the early 20th century. Once the tea industry was established, it was imperative to safeguard both the tea plants and the labour force from possible attacks by the hill tribes, some of whom reacted angrily against the occupation by outsiders of their traditional hunting territories. The British administration therefore sent peace missions to the hill regions. Not surprisingly, the rebellious tribes engaged the attention of officials more than those who were docile. The institutions and practices of some tribal groups were documented.

However, a thorough understanding of the tribes of Arunanchal Pradesh remained elusive until the anthropologist Christoph von Furer-Haimendorf carried out an extensive study during the 1930s. His research on the Apa Tani, in particular, has given us a full and vivid picture of their traditional way of life. They live in compact villages and became renowned for transforming their valley through intensive cultivation. The Nishis and the Hill Miris are their immediate neighbours. The Nishis were infamous for their lawlessness and their resistance to government-imposed order. The other tribes of the state are the Adi (Abor), Aka, Gallong, Khampti, Mishmi, Monpa, Nocte, Sherdukpen, Singpho, Tangsa and Wancho. In this chapter we will concentrate on the life and customs of the Nishi and the Aka.

The state of Arunachal Pradesh, which was earlier called the North-Eastern Frontier Agency (NEFA), covers an area of 81,424 square kilometres (31,437 square miles). According to the Census of India 1971 (which was the last time tribal figures were officially reported) the state

Old man of the Nishi tribe repairing a fishing net near the river.

had a population of 467,511. Arunachal Pradesh was the least densely populated area of India, it had a density of six people per square kilometre when the average was 178 people per square kilometre.

Before moving on to a description of the Nishi and the Aka, it might be useful to clarify the confusion that surrounds the names of these tribes. The British administrators kept the names given to the hill tribes by the plains dwellers. From their official publications, the tribes became known to the wider world by the names we are now familiar with. The term Naga, for example, which originally meant "naked", was used by the Assamese for the hill people living beyond Dimapur. Similarly, the term Dafla was used for the hill people of the western part of the present Subansiri district and the term Abor for the inhabitants of Siang district. Like the blanket term Naga, these terms also have pejorative connotations, meaning "wild man" or "barbarian".

Unfortunately, these terms were not only adopted by the British, but also by the Census officials and administrators of post-colonial India. With the spread of modern education and the strengthening of tribal sentiment, these derogatory titles have been rejected by the tribes themselves. The Nagas want to be identified by their specific tribal names, such as Angami, Ao, Chakesang, Sema and Rengma. The tribes previously identified as Dafla want to be called Nishi or Nishang, which are both terms derived from the word *ni*, which means "human being". Similarly, the term Abor has been replaced by Adi, meaning "indigene".

Old man of the Nishi tribe.
FOLLOWING DOUBLE PAGE: *A longhouse. Some of these longhouses are 60 metres long and shelter up to five families. In the foreground is a Nishi man wearing the* podum, *the tribe's characteristic hairstyle.*

The Nishi, whose current population exceeds 49,500, have traditionally been a martial people. Robinson (1851) classified the Nishi as Caucasians belonging to the Scythic race; Dalton (1872) however believed them to be Mongoloids. Furer-Haimendorf (1951) writes that most of Nishi have a round, flat-face with a broad snub-nose and a weak chin. They style their hair in a way similar to that of the people of Arunachal Pradesh. Their hair, 30 centimetres (1 foot) long, is passed horizontally through the bun (*podum*). The headdress is completed with a cane helmet with a crest depicting the beak of a hornbill. The cane helmet may have additional decorations, depending upon the person's status.

Men traditionally wear several rings around the waist, arms and legs, probably to protect themselves from sword cuts, flies and cold. They also wear a sleeveless, short, thick cotton cloth with blue and red stripes and a cloak of cotton or woollen cloth fastened around the throat and shoulders by means of pins. The chest is usually covered by a mithan (*Bos frontalis*, wild bison) hide, and several strings made of beads in varying sizes and colours are worn around the neck. Every Nishi warrior carries a *dao* (sword) and a knife, both sheathed in bamboo scabbards.

Nishi women wear a simple dress — a sleeveless mantle of striped or plain cloth tucked tightly over their chest covers the body from the armpits to the centre of the calves and fastened at the waist by ribbon threads. Their hair is parted in the middle, plaited and gathered into a chignon just above the nape. Nishi women also wear multicoloured bead necklaces, brass chains and metal bells, and adorn their wrists with heavy bracelets. The earlobes are extended, by inserting bamboo plugs in infancy, which are substituted by huge brass or silver rings when the girls grow up, stretching the earlobes to the shoulders.

According to Nishi tradition, the tribe is believed to have descended from a mythical ancestor named Takr. His sons became the forefathers of the three branches of the tribe, respectively, called Dopum, Dodum and Dol. Each of these branches is divided into several phratries, which are exogamous (i.e. they do not allow marriage inside the group), and these in turn are divided into clans. This system spreads over a large area, although in practice the knowledge of most men does not extend beyond their own phratries and clans. These Nishi kinship groups have never been political units, and their villages have never co-operated to pursue political goals. This has led some anthropologists to describe the Nishi "state" as lawless. It would more accurate to say that political centralisation has been impossible because of constant moves in search of secure and viable places in which to live. The primary social unit among the Nishi is the household. They are polygynous (i.e. men take more than one wife), and they usually live in longhouses, which sometimes run to over 60 metres (190 feet) in length. These longhouses differ from those found among the tribal groups of Borneo, in that Nishi houses are not subdivided into separate compartments as with those of the Ibans of Borneo. In the longhouses of the Nishi, every married woman has her own separate establishment. A small Nishi village has three or four houses; a large one may have around thirty. The individual houses are usually widely dispersed. Each longhouse is surrounded by granaries and pigsties and ideally stands on the highest point of a hillock. The members of a longhouse are under an obligation to support each other in any dispute with outsiders.

The warriors live in extended families and it is not unusual for 40 or 50 people to live in a single house, yet each married woman has a separate "kitchen" for herself and her children. Virtually forming an autonomous social unit, each house has a big undivided hall at the centre of which is fireplaces for cooking. The fireplace closest to the entrance door belongs to the head of the joint family, who is also the owner of the house. Following the rule of primogeniture, the fireplace is taken over by the eldest son when his father dies. The most senior wife of the headman has exclusive rights over this fireplace, where she cooks for her husband, herself and her children. Each of a man's other wives has a fireplace of her own. The husband always eats at the fireplace of his most senior wife, and it is also here that the food for his guests is cooked.

A Nishi family on the veranda of their longhouse.

Younger brothers of the owner of the house and their wives are allotted separated fireplaces, as is a son when married.

The walls of the houses are made of twill matting and the floor is covered with flattened bamboo. The most striking contribution of the Nishi to the domestic architecture of Arunachal Pradesh is the *tumco* balcony. The balcony, which is half-open and half-covered by a thatched roof, is located at the back of the house. It provides a convenient meeting place for members of the family and their guests, and is the place where rituals and sacrifices are performed.

The longhouses have no store rooms. Personal possessions such as clothes are kept covered in baskets suspended from the rafters or hung on the walls. Grain is stored in granaries and usually each woman and her unmarried children has a granary of her own. Spears, *daos*, and knives are stuck into wattle walls or simply hung up on rafters. Agricultural implements, such as hoes and digging sticks, are kept in a corner. The Nishi make many types of baskets, and they are also hung on the rafters, or placed on a tray kept hanging above the hearth.

Tibetan bells and bronze plates are the Nishi's most valuable possessions and are never usually kept in their houses. They are kept hidden or buried in a safe place in the forest. If a house accidentally catches fire or is set on fire by raiders, the Nishi say that they do not lose much, as a house can be built within a month or two, and the domestic and agricultural implements they need are easily acquired. There is plenty of timber near the Nishi villages to rebuild the houses. House construction is one of the activities in which all villages work together, the owner of the house providing beer and food to his helpers.

The longhouses have no store rooms. The Nishi do not have community houses like the men's dormitories (also referred to as "youth dormitories") found among the Naga tribes. The Naga dormitory, known as the *morung*, is a place where unmarried men socialise and work together. Furer-Haimendorf (1982:35) observes that the absence of a youth dormitory among the

A meal for the pigs in a Nishi village.
OPPOSITE PAGE: *A Nishi woman.*

Nishi is an indication that their society is "loosely structured, and without an organised system of authority extending beyond the limits of a simple longhouse," adding that the sense of discipline and esprit de corps that is instilled in the Naga youth in their dormitories is absent among the Nishi.

Traditional Nishi society has been largely characterised by instability and large-scale migration. This has largely been because there has not been a centralised political structure. The most important social units for the Nishi have been the longhouse and the village, rather than the loosely integrated tribe.

The instability of the Nishi may also be linked to the system of land tenure that provided for no individual rights to land. The inhabitants of a settlement were free to cultivate wherever they wanted, and as the people moved on, new pieces of land came under cultivation. Permanent settlement, and individual ownership of land that comes with it, played no part in Nishi society. Movable possessions, such as cattle or implements, were also likely to be stolen by raiders. Because of this prevailing insecurity and the frequency of raids, men could easily be enslaved by others for their own use or for sale to others. Such slaves and their children became members of the owner's longhouse but over time could seek freedom and acquire property. There was, thus, no permanent slave class as with the Apa Tanis.

Shifting cultivation is the only method of agriculture possible in the Nishi region. The forested slopes are cleared at altitudes between 300-1,800 metres (1,000-6,000 feet), and rice, millet and

PRECEDING DOUBLE PAGE: *A Nishi woman sorts grain.*

152

pulses cultivated using a hoe and the digging stick. Though they breed cattle, the Nishi do not use them to haul loads. Felling trees and other laborious jobs are done with the neighbour's help, and as with house construction, the helpers get beer and food from those they work for. When a man's neighbours help him clear the forest vegetation on the plot he plans to cultivate, he provides a pig, or even a bison (*mithan*), and large quantities of rice-beer for them to feast on.

The Nishi are divided into many clans and clan exogamy is observed when choosing a spouse. Marriages are never negotiated until the couples have attained maturity. As noticed earlier, the Nishi are polygynous, but not every man can acquire more than one wife, it depends upon his wealth, which is measured by the number of bison, pigs, clothes, swords, salt, fermented millet, and so on, he owns. A rich man may have as many as eight wives. The need to have additional hands for agricultural work is one of the most important reasons for polygyny.

As in many other societies, Nishis also have a system under which widows are inherited. Old widows are exempt from this rule and may continue to remain in the family without being inherited. Unmarried sons inherit the youngest of the widows, a son inherits the widows of his father with the exception of his natal mother. One advantage in widow inheritance is that the requirement to pay a dowry, normally necessary when acquiring a new wife, is dispensed with.

Nishi households may consist of others, apart from the married sons or brothers of the headman. There may also be dependents, not related by blood, who sought refuge in the house after being threatened or harmed by their enemies. If the head of the house has slaves, they will

Weaving with bamboo is a popular occupation among young Nishi women.

also be given separate fireplaces. Although the Nishi are patriarchal (i.e. continue to live in their father's house after marriage), in some exceptional cases, a daughter may be given a fireplace in her natal house or a son-in-law accommodated in his father-in-law's longhouse. The more kinsmen and dependents a man has in his longhouse, the more prestige he enjoys in the community. When a man is incapacitated, he may transfer his authority to his eldest son, but even then he remains the symbolic head, and his fireplace continues to be the closest to the front door. Only after his death does his position pass to his successor. This is in contrast to the elderly among the Apa Tani who, after relinquishing their house and authority to their son, move to a smaller house.

Nishi society, as noted before, was perennially threatened by raiders and this made it imperative that every man was a warrior. They were armed with a spear with an iron head, a large sword and a bow with poison arrows. In war, the chest and back were covered with a bison hide, a black cloak made of local fibre was worn over this, and a shield made of hide, formed a third protective layer.

In comparison to the Nishis, the Aka are a minor tribe. They are sub-divided into groups known as Kotsun, Kovatsun and Miri, and live in the sub-Himalayan region of Arunachal Pradesh. They are confined to 21 villages, of which Dijungania, Jamiri and Buragaon are the largest. In the last 100 years or so, their number have increased from 1,000 to 12,500.

The Aka are fair-skinned, well built, flat-nosed and have high Mongoloid cheek bones. The men tie their hair in a knot in the middle of their heads, while the women wear their hair at the back. The men's headdress is a round cane cap about 7.6 centimetres (3 inches) high with long feathers in front. They wear a long silk toga and leggings down to their ankles, and carry a sword of about 1.2 metres (4 feet) long in their cummerbunds. Women wear an ankle-length red garment. Those who are affluent wear a delicate silver chain around their heads. In their ears, they wear large vase-shaped silver earrings, and normally also several necklaces of coloured beads. Their jewellery and clothes are bought from Assam, and it is quite usual for women to tattoo their faces.

The home of an Aka is built on a 1.8 metre-high (6 feet) platform and divided into three compartments. The porch, which is used as a guestroom, is a special feature of their architecture. Bamboo, wooden planks and cane leaves constitute the building materials. The middle floor is where the pigs and goats are kept, and is also used as a lavatory. Granaries are built a little distance away from the main house.

Shifting cultivation is the only type of agriculture practised by the Aka. Once exhausted, the clearing is left fallow for seven or eight years, and then the seeds are sown by removing a little earth with a hoe and planting them underneath. Temporary huts are built near the crops so that wild animals can be scared away. The staple diet of the Aka is maize and millet, with pulses, potatoes and French beans as supplements (milk does not form part of their diet). They partake of three varieties of alcoholic drink. There is a mild beverage called *laopani*; a stronger drink called *mingri* which is consumed daily; and a special drink called *arrah*, a luxury that only the well-to-do can afford on a daily basis. All three are prepared from fermented maize and millet.

Aka society is based on a patriarchal residence and the law of primogeniture. The household consists of a husband and wife, their unmarried children and slaves. A special hut is built for women to live in when they are menstruating. The marriageable age for men is around 20, and for girls between 15 and 20. In a ceremonial marriage, the priest (*mugou*) declares the auspicious period to open marriage negotiations. Then a go-between (*mukhou*) is entrusted with the task of match-making, fixing the amount of dowry and the date of the wedding. His fee is an iron hearth stand (*aeschperi*). The auspicious days for the wedding are found by looking at the indigenous calendar, which is made by tying a series of knots on a cane string. Each seventh knot represents an auspicious day.

*A Nishi family in the kitchen of their longhouse. Since there are no enclosures in the longhouses,
every married woman has a small corner to herself.*
BELOW: *An old Dafla smoking a carved bamboo and silver pipe.*

Clan exogamy is also observed among the Aka who intermarry with their neighbours, the Miji. Marriage with a "cross" cousin (i.e. with a father's sister's daughter or a mother's brother's daughter) is preferred. But it is also possible to marry a "parallel" cousin (i.e. a father's brother's daughter or a mother's sister's daughter). Like some other tribes of Arunachal Pradesh, the Aka are also polygamous. Sister polygamy, where a man is married to two sisters is preferred. A widow may marry her husband's elder brother, a widower may take his deceased wife's younger sister in marriage.

The marriage ceremony is very colourful. The groom's party brandish their *dao* while approaching the bride's house in response to a similar display by the host's party. A mimicked fight then ensues in which the bride's party always concedes defeat. The young women of the bride's village blacken the faces of the groom's friends and the boys reciprocate in kind. The older women dress up like men. After the marriage, the bridegroom remains for a year as a visiting husband in his bride's house before finally taking her away to his father's home.

Elopement, because of parental objection, is common. When the lovers reach the village of the groom's parent a pig is sacrificed and the villagers are invited to a feast where the news is announced. The local priest then ties a thread made of sheep hair (*fokki*) around the girl's wrist and this makes the marriage binding. The dowry is one or two bison, one iron hearth stand and a set of clothes. The dowry is normally payable at the time of marriage, but it can also be paid afterwards. In case of elopement, cohabitation is permitted only after the marriage payments have been settled.

The Aka always bury their dead. A small stone building around 1.2 metres (4 feet) in height is built over the body. An altar made of split wood, streaked with blue and smeared with the blood of a chicken is placed near the body, as are the clothes, utensils and weapons of the dead person.

The entire village mobilises to build a longhouse.
It will take five more days to complete this house.

Observers of the northeastern tribal world think that the Aka, who used to be "bold and daring", are now a "peace-loving people". Predatory incursions, tribal feuds and internecine wars are no longer undertaken. At one time, the Aka were subject to domination by another tribal group, the Bangni, who exacted tribute from them under the threat of raids. In turn, the Aka exerted pressure of their Sherdukpen neighbours as well as the Khowa. Such tribal rivalries are now at an end following the impact of tribal development programmes instituted by the Arunanchal Pradesh government. Some of the customs and practices of the Aka have also changed because of Hindu and Buddhist influence in their homeland.

A Nishi woman crosses a bamboo bridge.
OPPOSITE PAGE: *A Nishi wearing a cloak of plant fibres.*

A Nishi fisherman midstream.
OPPOSITE PAGE: *Tobacco being exchanged en route to the market.*

A Nishi warrior wearing a cloak of plant fibres and sporting a traditional podum *hairstyle.*
The shoulder strap for his sword is made of monkey's hair, and the sheath is of bamboo.

Prayers
In The Wind

Gautama Buddha received enlightenment when meditating under a banyan tree in Gaya, a small town in the state of Bihar. His teachings of tolerance, kindness and compassion spread throughout the Indian subcontinent. The great King Ashoka embraced these teachings, thus giving state patronage to Buddhism, and in the following centuries they were carried to neighbouring kingdoms by monks. By 220BC, the influence of Buddhism was felt as far away as China.

Buddhist monks travelled far and wide, spreading their faith. Most of the isolated hill communities accepted their teachings and provided assistance in building monasteries. In Tibet, Buddhism thrived until the mid-1950s when its followers and monks were persecuted by the Chinese government. In 1959, the temporal and religious head of Tibet, the Dalai Lama, along with thousands of his followers, fled Lhasa, the state capital, to seek refuge in India. The refugees settled all over India, ranging from Dharamsala in the north to as far south as Mundgod in Mysore (Karnataka). The Dalai Lama established his monastery in Dharamsala (Himachal Pradesh).

Today, Tibetan Buddhism is one of the principal forms of Buddhism in India, as indigenous Indian Buddhism died out many centuries ago because of the Muslim invasions and the spread of Hinduism. Besides the Tibetan settlers, however, there are two other types of community that are identified as Buddhist in the Censuses of India. First, there are several tribes in the Himalayas

Statue of the Buddha in the Tawang Monastery (Arunachal Pradesh).
OPPOSITE PAGE: *Prayer batons in Monpa country (Arunachal Pradesh).*
FOLLOWING DOUBLE PAGE: *Traditional wooden house of the Monpa tribe (Arunachal Pradesh).*

who we will look at in this chapter. Secondly, there are those communities, designated as neo-Buddhist, who embraced Buddhism under the influence of Dr. B.R. Ambedkar, the chief architect of the Constitution of India. Himself a member of a low caste (Mahar), Ambedkar fought for the rights of untouchables. One way to escape the scourge of the caste system, he thought, was to embrace an egalitarian religion such as Buddhism. Under his leadership, some of the untouchable communities, such as the Mahars of Maharashtra and Jatavs of Agra, adopted Buddhist beliefs. Neo-Buddhism is essentially an anti-caste political movement occurring among Hindu plains people rather than India's tribes.

The Buddhist tribes all have links with Tibet. Some of them claim to have migrated from there. Others have been trading for centuries with Tibetan merchants, and through contact with them have become converted to Buddhism. The type of Buddhism they practice though is interwoven with local traditions and institutions, and differs from classical Buddhism in several ways. In some cases, Buddhism coexists with the cults of pre-Buddhist deities. Buddhist monks sometimes officiate at cult rituals of local deities, for example among the Jad Bhotia of Uttarkashi district (Uttar Pradesh). Some scholars refer to the Buddhism of Tibet and the Himalayas as Lamaism because of the central position monks (lamas) occupy in this religion.

One Buddhist tribe lives in Zanskar Valley in the Himalayas. Zanskar means "The Land of White Copper" and is administratively part of the state of Jammu and Kashmir. The Zanskaris have their own language, customs, traditions, history and king. According to Tibetan texts, the Zanskari kingdom was founded in AD930.

Apart from a travel account by Michel Peissel (1979), virtually nothing is known about Zanskar. This is not surprising as it is one of the highest and most inaccessible areas of the world. The only outsiders to be found in the valley are government officials, who never number more than half a dozen. Existing at a mean altitude of 4,050 metres (13,500 feet), the Zanskar

A Monpa woman wearing a traditional five-pointed felt cap.
OPPOSITE PAGE: *A Monpa woman knitting wool.*
FOLLOWING DOUBLE PAGE: *A woman weaving outside her house.*

Valley is 320 kilometres (200 miles) long. In the mid-1970s when Peissel visited it, the valley had 28 villages and a population of around 12,000.

The Zanskari economy is self-sufficient and not based on money. The chief crop is barley, and cows and goats are domesticated. The people weave their own clothes and make their own footwear. Each family has its own field which they cultivate. For activities requiring additional labour, neighbours help on a reciprocal basis. Every village has its own pastures in the valley and the mountains, where the herds are grazed in summer. In higher villages, barley is the only crop grown, while in the lower villages there is a system of rotating crops. The order of crop rotation is generally peas, barley and wheat. Zanskari houses have a vegetable garden in which onions, radishes, cucumbers and potatoes are grown.

Peissel observed that every Zanskari woman wore all her jewellery even when engaged in daily household activities. This habit had its origins in more uncertain times, when villages had to flee to different areas to avoid raiders. The women's jewellery consists of ornaments studded with precious stones imported from Tibet and Afghanistan.

There are four sects of Tibetan Buddhism. The oldest of these is Nyingmapa, the word nying meaning old. This sect adheres both to the classical texts and to those "revealed" to the monks. Elements of the pre-Buddhist magical religion called Bon have also been incorporated in the beliefs of the Nyingmapa sect. In the Sakyapa sect, there has been a very deliberate effort to eliminate all magical practices. A third sect, known as the Kargyapa (also called Red Hat), accepts some of the Nyingmapa texts but not others. Finally, there is the Gelugpa (Yellow Hat) sect whose leaders were temporal rulers of Tibet (until 1959) and religious rulers of Buddhist kingdoms in central Asia.

The Zanskari monasteries belong to the Yellow Hat and the Red Hat sects and they coexist peacefully. The monks not only carry out their daily rituals and study, but are also available for

A Monpa tribesman weaving bamboo to cover the roof of his house before it snows..

any spiritual guidance the people require. The fierce divinities from the Hindu pantheon have found their way into Tibetan Buddhism, and are often seen painted on the walls of monasteries. Throughout the Himalayas there is a pervasive belief that they should be pacified, for they are dangerous and can cause irreparable damage to people and their belongings.

According to the present inhabitants of Zanskar, they came originally from Amdo, an eastern district of Tibet. It is also said that a young Zanskari man once went to Amdo where he came upon a big lake. As he was looking at it, a beautiful woman emerged. The two were married and had many children. Their progeny, it is said, live in Amdo and so there exists a kinship between the two settlements.

The Monpa of Arunachal Pradesh also claim to have originated in Tibet. They live in the western part of Kameng district and number around 30,000 They are of Mongoloid stock, and speak a Tibeto-Burmese dialect. Their physical features, dress, ornaments and some of their cultural practices, resemble those of the people of eastern Bhutan. Their area is divided into three main regions: Tawang, Dirang and Kalaktang.

Tawang, the most populous of these areas, was first influenced by Buddhism in the 11th century. The first monasteries were established by monks of the Kargyapa and Nyingmapa sects. But when the Gelugpa sect was firmly entrenched in Tibet, one of its monks (Mera Lama) set out for the Tawang Valley to spread their doctrine. With the help of the fifth Dalai Lama (1617-82), a magnificent Yellow Hat monastery was founded. It is claimed that a horse led the founder

Monpa houses (Tawang, Arunachal Pradesh).
FOLLOWING DOUBLE PAGE: *Monpa weaving bamboo for the house's roof.*

to the monastery's site; thus the full name of the Tawang Monastery is Celestial Paradise of the Divine Site chosen by a Horse.

As the monks lived on alms, the Tawang Monpa agreed to pay a grain tax for the upkeep of the monastery and its monks. A revenue officer was appointed to collect it and since its inception, the tax has never been revised. The obligation to pay it is passed from father to son. Today, around 110 Tawang villages pay the tax. Every monk has the right to a share in the monastery store which is collectively owned.

Furer-Haimendorf (1982:166) contrasts this system with the monasteries of Nepal, where the monks depend on the contributions they receive from their respective families. There, normally, a poor man cannot afford to enter the monastic life unless someone agrees to provide him with subsistence. Rich monks, in this way, sometimes act as patrons. A Tawang monk has another privilege: he is permitted to hold private property, such as land and animals, and retain any income they provide. The Tawang Monastery also has a paper mill, and once had a printing press where Tibetan texts were printed. All these texts are still housed in the monastery's library. According to Furer-Haimendorf (1982:166) in 1980 Tawang Monastery was home to 265 monks, but rarely were all of them there at the same time. Once every three years, however, when the monastery is repaired and painted, all the monks come together.

The Monapa used to trade with the adjoining provinces of Tibet but after the closure of the mountain passes by the government, they have turned their attention to agriculture. They grow rice on irrigated fields, and maize, millet, wheat and barley are cultivated on dry fields. Shifting cultivation is also practised on steep slopes where terracing is difficult. Their ploughs are drawn by a hybrid bison (jiatsa), which is a cross between the indigenous species of bison and Indian cattle. The ploughs are large and heavy and need to be worked by two men.

A Monpa Woman.
OPPOSITE PAGE: *A Monpa bathroom at 3,800 metres (12,464 feet) and a few degrees below zero.*

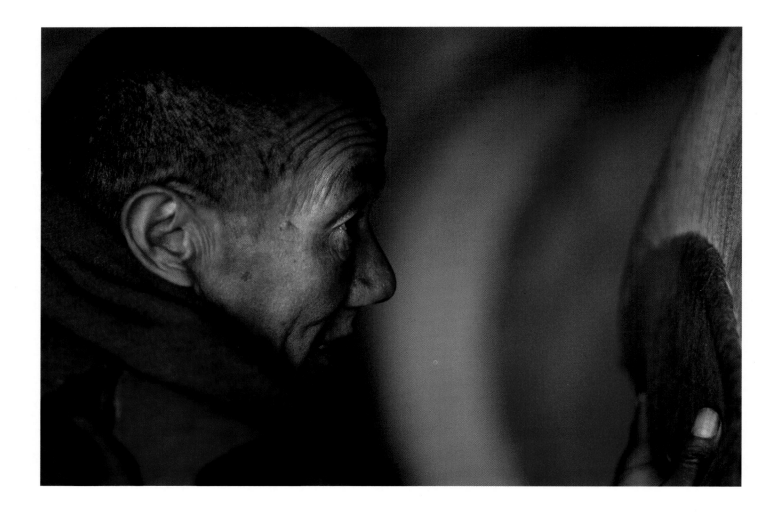

As well as farming the land, the Monpa rear bison, cows, pigs, sheep and goats and, in the high altitude villages, yaks. In most villages they keep bees and also collect wild honey. Before roads were constructed, horses used to be the main form of transport. Some of the Monpa villages still breed and sell horses. Sheep are reared primarily for meat rather than wool. Unlike the other tribes in the state, they milk their cows every morning to feed their children.

The Monpa make carpets, mats and saddlebags. They also make wooden images of Lord Buddha, while the influence of Buddhist iconography is clearly visible in their textiles, ornaments and architecture. They say that their society changed with the coming of Buddhism. For example, the system of elected headmen came into being because they needed responsible figures to oversee the maintenance of monasteries. However, in recent years, the government has appointed headmen (*gaonburras*, literally, the "old men of the village") who arbitrate all disputes on traditional lines.

The institution of polyandry exists among the Monpas. Pre-marital sex is permitted, and young people are usually left to find a spouse for themselves. The marriage itself, however, is arranged by the patrilineal clans of the bride and groom. A dowry usually consists of a horse and a yak, and a dowry is also given to the daughter by her parents when she moves to her husband's house. Should the marriage fail, and the girl decide to return to her natal village, the dowry is returned in its entirety.

Family property is usually divided by the head of the household before his death. The largest share goes to the eldest son, and the parents continue to live with him. Because of this, an eldest son is never permitted to go and live with his wife's parents as a resident son-in-law (*makba*). His younger brothers may choose to live as makba, but should they do so, they lose all their rights to their parents' property. Like the Zanskaris, the Monpa combine Buddhist and Bon practices. Indeed, in all the Himalayan Buddhist tribes there is the co-existence of these two

Monks at Tawang Monastery (Arunachal Pradesh).
The Dalai Lama rested here on his journey into exile.

different ideologies and practices. The Monpa believe that the local spirits need to be placated, but at the same time they hold that merit can only be earned by meditation and carrying out practical acts, such as making a prayer-wheel for the monastery or donating labour for the construction of a road.

Monpa villages have stone platforms dedicated to local spirits. Incense sticks are burnt here, and on specific occasions, animal sacrifices are performed and offerings of beer are made. These local deities have their own priests (*bun*) who have no connection with the Buddhist monks. In addition, the Monpa villages have shamans (*yu-min*) who are possessed by gods and spirits.

The other Buddhist tribe of Arunachal Pradesh is the Khova. They also live in Kemang district. Living in ten villages, their population, according to the 1971 Census of India, was 703. Very little information is available about them since no anthropologist has yet studied them in detail. However, both Furer-Haimendorf (1982a, b) and Elwin (1965) mention them in passing, giving us a glimpse into their lives. The Khova call themselves Bugun in their own language. Until recently, they used to practice shifting cultivation. They do not use the plough when farming, perhaps because they have hardly any level land. They rear cattle by cross-breeding the local species of bison with Indian cattle.

The Khova are divided into exogamous clans, but strictly observe the rule of not marrying outside the tribe. Like the traditional religion of other tribes in this region, the Khova also have an elaborate system of gods and nature spirits who are gratified with animal sacrifices. In recent

A child and his horse at Tawang Monastery (Arunachal Pradesh).
OPPOSITE PAGE: *A hand-built wall with prayers to the wind en route to Tawang.*

A young Zanskari girl carrying wood.
OPPOSITE PAGE: *Chorten (Zanskar).*

years, the influence of Tibetan Buddhism on them has been very marked and they have started seeking out Buddhist monks to officiate at their rituals. In 1982, Furer-Haimendorf wrote that the Khova had a plan to build a monastery in one of their villages, and that they had also decided to send some of their boys to seek training under Bhutanese monks.

In comparison to the Zanskaris and the tribes from Arunachal Pradesh, not all the Bhotia can be classified as Buddhist. In the eastern Himalayas, they follow this faith, but in the central Himalayas, they are either Hindus or continue to practice their traditional religion. In fact, the term Bhotia designates several different groups of people in the Himalayan and trans-Himalayan regions: even the people of Bhutan are often referred to as Bhotia. Confusion arises because in different districts they call themselves by different names. For example, in Pithoragarh, they call themselves Shouka; in Chamoli they adopt the name of Marcha; and in Uttarkashi, they identify themselves as Jad. Some scholars prefer to classify them geographically into western and eastern Bhotia, while some take language as the best index of identification, contrasting Tibeto-Burmese speaking Bhotia with those who speak an Indo-Aryan dialect.

There is however no ambiguity about one thing: at one time all Bhotia were involved in some form of trade between Tibet and the region where they lived. They carried whatever goods were available in their own areas to Tibetan markets and exchanged them for salt, borax and wood. Traditionally, they sold rice, wheat, barley, sugar, jaggary, tobacco, and many other house-hold goods, establishing a complete monopoly on transborder trade. Over the generations, their

A Kowa woman (Arunachal Pradesh).
OPPOSITE PAGE: *An old Monpa man wearing the traditional five-pointed cap.*

trade flourished and many became rich. When trade was at its peak, they were the most prosperous and forward-looking people in the area. They used to spend the summer in Tibetan markets, arriving there after several days of travel with teams of ponies and yaks, which carried their goods. Winter was spent on the plains buying articles to be taken to Tibet the following summer.

Trading was supplemented by rearing animals. They domesticated goats and sheep, the male animals being sold in the markets along with woollen products. They owned large estates of land but never tilled them themselves. The task of cultivation was normally given over to peasant castes from whom a rent was exacted in the form of a share of the harvest. Because of their economic prosperity, the Bhotia had a superior status in multi-caste villages. Socially, they were considered members of warrior caste (the Rajput), although they never actually married members of Hindu castes themselves.

While their trade suffered greatly because of the Chinese occupation of Tibet, they nevertheless continued to trade with their counterparts on the other side of the Himalayas. The Sino-Indian War of 1962 changed all that, however, as it resulted in the permanent sealing of the Tibetan border. In the same year, the Bhotia had to face another traumatic change. The Uttar Pradesh government brought in a land act abolishing big estates to ease distribution of land to landless peasants. With the implementation of this act, most Bhotia land passed to their tenants. Now, most of them are obliged to work on whatever land they have left, farming or rearing animals. Some Bhotia have started to make carpets. Those who are educated are seeking jobs in both the private and government sectors. These changes, J.S. Bhandari says (1981:216), will deeply affect the social organisation of the Bhotia and their relationship with other groups and communities.

Kowa tribeswomen's traditional jewellery.
OPPOSITE PAGE: *A Kowa tribeswoman dressed in silver beads, reliquary and bracelets of silver, turquoise and coral.*

THE SHAMANS
OF THE
RICE VALLEY

D
ivination is a means of looking into the future and of identifying the causes of inexplic-
able illness and problems. Literally meaning "inspired by the divine force", divination
may be broadly classified into two types: inspirational and non-inspirational. When a
shaman practices inspirational divination, he is possessed by an animate or inanimate spirit,
which speaks through him. It may be the spirit of a dead ancestor, an animal, a plant, or even
that of lakes and mountains. The type of spirit in which people have faith depends on their cultural knowledge. Both the cause of problem and the means of alleviating it are suggested during
the trance the shaman falls into. By contrast, in non-inspirational divination, the diviner relies on
methods and omens that do not change his state of mind. Making predictions by observing the
movement of birds, or on the basis of astrological charts are two examples of non-inspirational
divination.

Both these types of divination are practised by Indian tribes. Elwin (1950:133) observed
"Altars with witch-baffling decorations, temporary booths, a great pother with leaf-cups, plates
and little bundles, grass dolls and wooden carts to carry away disease, the casting of rice to the
four quarters of the globe, offerings at hearth and threshold, protective gestures of waving and
sprinkling, taboos on looking back, going in or out, speaking to strangers, these are the common

A mithan prepared for sacrifice.
OPPOSITE PAGE: *An Apa Tani priest at the Morom Festival celebrating fertility rites
in winter to mark the beginning of the new agricultural cycle.*
FOLLOWING DOUBLE PAGE: *An Apa Tani village amid the rice fields.*

materials of religion and magic all over tribal and near-Hindu India. The Apa Tani of Arunachal Pradesh are a tribe famous for their shamans. The chapter offers an account of their life, concentrating on their religion and shamanism.

The Apa Tani live in seven villages in a fertile valley of about 20 square kilometres (8 square miles) in Subansiri district. In 1897, their population was estimated at around 5,000, today it is just under 11,000. Very little is known about the early history of the Apa Tani. However, their oral history and folklore indicates that even before they settled in the valley in Subansiri, they had a common ethnic identity. Every observer of the Apa Tani has been impressed by their unity and the compactness of their settlements, which are in sharp contrast to their neighbours in other districts of Arunachal Pradesh. It is said that they came from a land located somewhere in the north. A place known as Mudu Buru figures in their accounts, and they claim to have brought a species of plum tree from there, which remains of great ritual and ceremonial significance to this day. Another tree believed to have been brought by their ancestors is the pine (Pinus excelsa), which is a characteristic feature of the Subansiri Valley, but completely non-existent in the neighbouring Nishi area.

Unlike their neighbours — the Nishi and the Miri — the Apa Tani are generally regarded as a peace-loving, settled tribe. The Nishi (see Chapter 5) were always engaged in feuds, and had to move constantly in search of secure places to live. Whereas the Nishi and the Hill Miri tend to merge, one with the other, the Apa Tani constitute a separate endogamous group. They practice the most modern methods of terrace cultivation, and are famed for having transformed their valley through rice cultivation and irrigated terrace fields. Though cultivation has been the mainstay of their economy, animal traction was unknown to them until 1945. Captain G.M. Dun's statement in 1893 that "most of them till their fields with sharpened bamboo; a few only have acquired iron hoes" is still valid.

An Apa Tani house of woven bamboo.
OPPOSITE PAGE: *The Apa Tani's rice fields. They have cultivated every centimetre of the valley for centuries.*
FOLLOWING DOUBLE PAGE: *The bamboo huts of an Apa Tani village.*

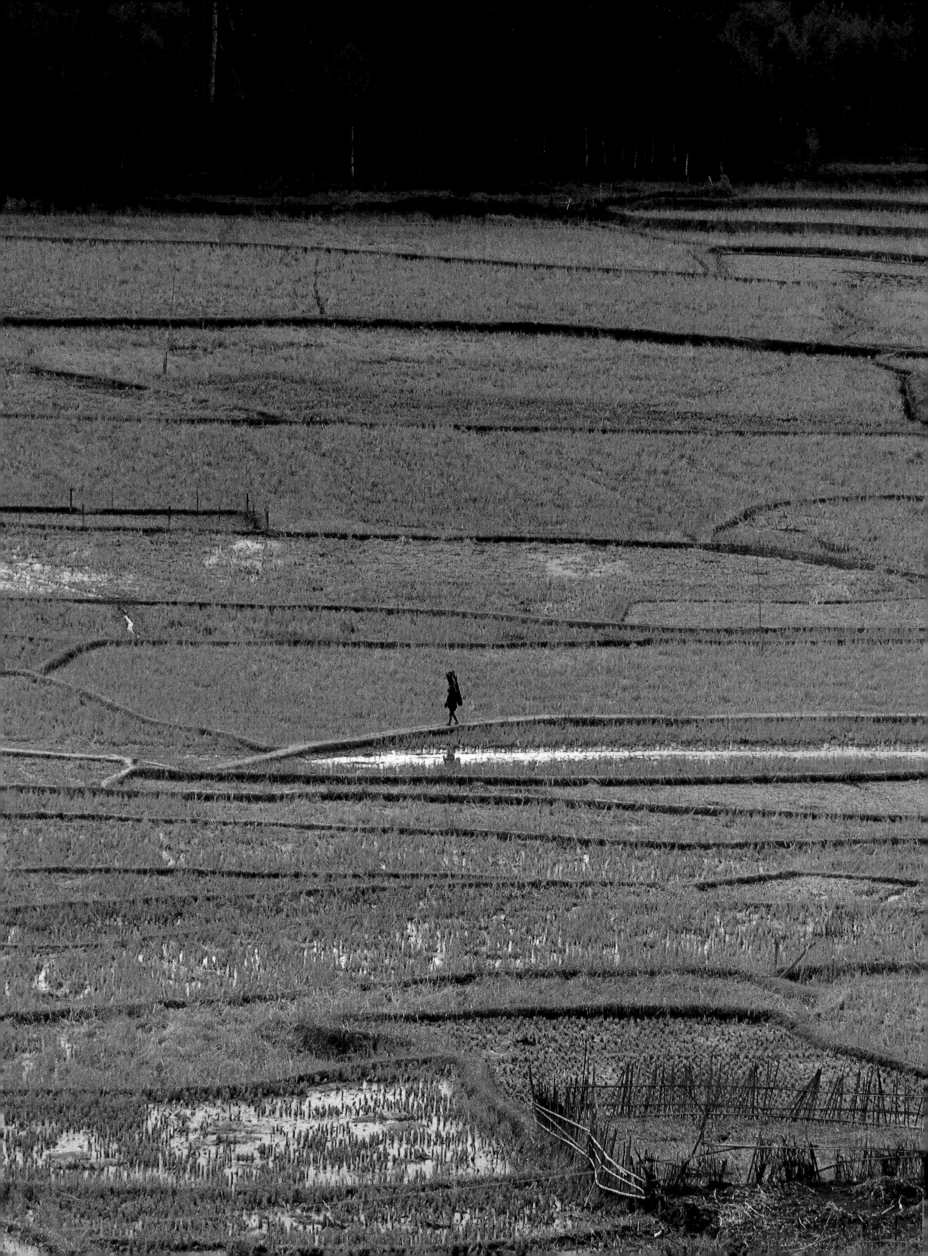

Their rice fields are either immersed permanently in water or allowed to dry out and harden after the harvest. Millet is their second most important crop. Although primarily used for brewing beer, millet is also ground into flour to make bread. In addition, the Apa Tani also cultivate three varieties of maize. Furer-Haimendorf (1980:33) comments that: "In view of the fact that maize, a crop indigenous in America, is believed to be a relatively late introduction in south Asia, it is remarkable that all three varieties are known by names which do not suggest a derivation from Indian or foreign words."

In contrast to the dispersed settlements of the Nishis, the Apa Tani's houses are clustered along well laid-out streets. All houses in the traditional style are of about the same width and are concentrated in the centre of the village. Every village has an open assembly platform called a lapang that is used for the performance of rituals and public gatherings. Men may be seen here making baskets, plaiting mats, carving wooden implements, or repairing other material objects. Apa Tani houses are constructed with bamboo and pinewood, both of which are abundant in their homeland. The roofs are thatched with paddy-straw.

Of Paleo-mongoloid stock, the Apa Tani have fair skin, prominent noses, deep-set eyes and long faces. The men wear their hair tied in a knot just above their foreheads and through the knot they pass a brass rod of about 30 centimetres (12 inches). They also wear a girdle of cane-work, which is painted red and hangs down from their backs in the form of a long bushy tail. Tattooing is common — typically a horizontal line is drawn across the under lip and straight lines are drawn downwards from this to the point of the chin.

The women insert wooden plugs into their nostrils. Small pegs are put in when they are little girls, and as they grow up, the size of the pegs are progressively increased until they are about 5-7.5 centimetres (2-3 inches) in diameter. The women are tattooed with broad blue lines that

A woman wearing a characteristic wooden nose ornament.
OPPOSITE PAGE: *Narrow pathway in an Apa Tani village.*
FOLLOWING DOUBLE PAGE: *Daybreak in the Apa Tani Valley.*

run from the top of the forehead to the tip of the nose, and then from lower lip to the top of the chin. Generally, five vertical lines are tattooed on the base of the chin. Their usual hairstyle is not particularly distinctive: the tresses are gathered up and rolled into two balls at the side of the head. A brass skewer is inserted horizontally through these to hold them in place.

Before Indian independence, there was no money in circulation among the Apa Tani. Even today, the wealth of an Apa Tani is measured primarily by the number of domesticated bison he owns. This animal's traditional habitat extends from Akaran and Burma throughout Nagaland and Arunachal Pradesh as far as Bhutan. Indeed, the bison plays a central role in the lives of all the tribes of northeast India. The bison head forms the state symbol of Nagaland, and the gates in Naga villages have carved bison heads at their centre.

As late as the 1940s, the bison was the recognised currency in all transactions concerning land. The price of a full-grown bison was 30 baskets of paddy, each weighing 27 kilograms (60 pounds). A house site could be purchased with no less than ten bison; a site for storing grain could be bought in exchange for a small bison. The cost of a large bamboo grove was three bison, and that of a terraced paddy field of half an acre, ten bison. Now, though, with the introduction of a cash economy, the bison is seldom used as currency.

The bison has, however, remained the principal sacrificial animal. It is slaughtered on many ritual occasions, such as the so-called "feast of merit". When people compete for social prestige, they slaughter a bison rather any other domestic animal. Ransoms and fines are usually settled by transferring bison to the respective parties. Though a dowry is not obligatory in Apa Tani society, as is the case among the Nishi and the Aka, the rich usually pay five or more bison when a marriage takes place. This practice is believed to enhance their prestige.

Distribution of rice flour blessed by the priest.
PRECEDING DOUBLE PAGE: *After the harvest, Apa Tani women carrying rice in bamboo baskets for the Morom Festival (fertility rites).*
OPPOSITE PAGE: *Rice that will be used for preparing alcohol for the Morom Festival.*

The Apa Tani are notorious in anthropological literature for their institution of slavery, which was widespread before Indian independence in 1947. Although other tribes of Arunachal Pradesh, like the Nishi, had status distinctions, they were not as extreme as those of the Apa Tani.

Apa Tani society was divided into nobles (*mite, guth*) and slaves (*mura, guchi*). Certain ethnic characteristics mirrored this division: a noble was distinguished by his tall stature, light skin, prominent nose and deep-set eyes, whereas a slave had more Mongoloid features. Upward mobility of slaves was impossible: a slave could become rich, but never rise in social status. Marriage between the two strata was absolutely ruled out, although love affairs between male slaves and girls of the nobility were possible. Slaves were usually sold to acquire bison when a ransom had to be paid for the return of a captured relative. They were also sold when cattle were required for ceremonial feasting. An adult slave normally fetched three to five bison.

If, on the one hand, the distinctions between the strata were marked and privileges well defined, on the other hand, there were certain "redeeming features", as Furer-Haimendorf (1980:17) calls them, of the Apa Tani's institution of slavery. No distinction was made between a slave and the son of his master in terms of the essentials of life such as food, shelter and clothing. The relation between a slave and his master was couched in the language of kinship; if the master was considerably older, the slave addressed him as "father", and if he was younger, "younger brother" was used. A slave was permitted to take part in public amusements and entertainment. Female slaves were not taken as concubines by their masters. Ties between the master and his slaves were characterised by paternalism. The master was not only responsible for the welfare of his slaves, but also conferred on them his own clan name.

An important difference noted by Furer-Haimendorf (1980:17) between the slaves of the Nishi and those of the Apa Tani was that an Apa Tani slaves, even when freed by their masters, remained economically dependent upon their masters. Nishi slaves could not only achieve freedom, but also own property, and gain the status of respected free men. Although the institution of slavery has been abolished, the erstwhile distinctions between the strata are still recognised, and any evidence of trespassing across social boundaries arouses strong feelings of anger among the Apa Tani.

Knowledge of this social hierarchy is crucial in an understanding of religious roles in Apa Tani society. It is these traditional roles that have changed least. Though they do not classify their gods in a hierarchy, there are several types of gods, each with their own specific characteristics. Communication with the gods and spirits is the prerogative of the priests (*nyibu*), who learn their skills during a lengthy training. Not everyone can become a priest. The Apa Tani believe that only members of the noble class have the right to acquire the skills needed to invoke gods and spirits.

Furer-Haimendorf (1980:150) writes, "There passes no day in the Apa Tani Valley without one or another priest approaching gods and spirits on behalf of individuals." Assistance is sought from supernatural powers on every important occasion, be it an illness or the construction of a house. The spirits are appeased collectively after a fire has destroyed any part of an Apa Tani village. Even today, when changes have occurred in someone's economic or social life, it is not uncommon to see the priests, dressed in ceremonial robes, carrying out rituals in individual houses or on open assembly platforms.

No temples or shrines are dedicated to the gods. Public rituals are carried out on the assembly platforms, while the venue for the performance of private rituals is a special corner of the house. The Apa Tani have two main public festivals called Morom and Moloka (or meek). Both of these are associated with the onset of the agricultural season. The Mormon sacrificial rites are similar to the Naga's feast of merit. Tribesmen who hold feasts for their kinsmen and neighbours enhance their prestige and status in the local community.

Apa Tani drinking alcohol made from rice.

Like the feast of merit in other tribal groups, the Apa Tani have different grades of feast. Three grades are usually distinguished. A simple morom rite is called ningsere and only a couple of bison, or a bison and a cow, are sacrificed. The meat is distributed to the donor's mother's brothers and father's mother's brothers. The second grade of rites is called *takum-puttu*. When these three bison are sacrificed, the giver of these feasts visits other villages and distributes the meat. In the highest order of these rites, referred to by the term *rung-ti* (or *guamopido*), four or five or even more, bison are sacrificed, and the donor's procession visits all the Apa Tani villages distributing the meat.

When a Nagas tribesman holds a feast he acquires some tangible privileges. He gains the right to decorate his house with bison horns and wear special clothes or ornaments, which both signify his elevated status. Furthermore, the office of a *goonbura* (village headman) for instance was generally allocated to the feast-giver, so that he acquires a considerable measure of social prestige and wealthy people always aspire to give such feasts. Those who are wealthy, but do not do give feasts are publicly criticised for being miserly. In effect, the feasts of merit function to level the wealth in a community.

The morom rites are celebrated at the end of winter before the beginning of agricultural work. The second set of public rites, *mloko*, coincide with the flowering of the fruit trees. These rites cannot begin before a ritually important plum tree has started flowering, usually in the middle of March. The mloko rites are performed collectively by villages in the same group. Preparations for the festivities begin several weeks earlier, they include purchase of sacrificial animals, the collection of firewood and the erection of tall poles. At the time of the rites, these poles are used for a game of acrobatics called "rope-swinging game". The Apa Tani play this game to entertain the gods attending the feast. The chief gods propitiated during the mloko rituals are a divine couple known as Kiru and Kilo. These rites are held annually by one or other of the villages belonging to a single group.

The priest's assistant.
OPPOSITE PAGE: *An Apa Tani woman and her child.*

The priest celebrates Morom rituals on a lapang, *a prayer
platform that symbolises the social cohesion of the clan.
The rituals continue all day, from 4am to 6pm.*

A mithan *prepared for sacrifice.*

These two rites *morom* and *mloko* are of crucial social importance. Furer-Haimendorf (1980) also recorded a number of other minor rituals that are performed by priests on behalf of individual villages. For example, in June or July, a small pig, a dog and some chickens are sacrificed to please the three deities believed to dwell on earth. In July or August, a chicken and eggs are offered to the god of thunder. Some rites are performed in order to ensure a plentiful rice harvest. Rites are also carried out when a leopard has been killed by a tribesman. The same rites are performed when an enemy has been slain. According to the Apa Tani, these rites prevent the soul of the dead enemy or animal from returning to the world. If this were to happen, they would take revenge on their killer.

Gods and spirits are believed to be invisible to ordinary people, but priests are endowed with the power to see them. There are myriad supernatural beings, but the generic term for all of them is *ui*. Though all gods and spirits are supposed to be equally important, in recent years the cult of Doni-Polo (Sun-Moon) has gained a particular significance for the Apa Tani. Furer-Haimendorf (1980) writes that this cult does not figure in their traditional religion. It is the educated tribes people who regard Doni-Polo as higher gods and are encouraging their worship. They believe that this cult can be used to unite the different Apa Tani villages of Subansiri district, thus giving the tribe a distinct identity. The importance of this cult in Subansiri can be gauged from the fact that it has been supported by the state government as a counter-force against Christianity and Buddhism. There are many examples of such indigenous cults in other tribal areas, and they often have great significance in tribal revivalist movements.

The gods worshipped by the Apa Tani may be classified into three categories according to their respective characteristics. The gods associated with happiness, prosperity and fecundity are called Tigo-ui. They are worshipped at all auspicious ceremonies, such as those performed during morom, mloko and marriages. Then there are spirits (called *Guninyon-ui* or *Chiching-ui*) connected with inauspicious and unfortunate events such as illness, accident, fire, and so on. A sacrifice is always performed to placate these spirits when a house in the village has been gutted by fire. The third kind of spirits, locally known as Yalu-ui, are connected with disputes and war. They are invoked before organising raids, or when crimes or kidnappings take place.

The Tigo-ui are benevolent spirits because they are invoked on auspicious occasions and should not therefore be brought into contact with those spirits which bring bad luck or are fierce by nature. However, the spirits connected with bad luck and those of war and raids may come in contact with each other because, by and large, they are of similar nature. The rituals dealing with any of the auspicious and benevolent spirits can be performed by married people only. However, those who are unmarried, widowed or separated may commission rituals for the spirits of bad luck and war.

In addition to these spirits, the Apa Tani believe in certain other deities who are associated with natural phenomena. To pacify them or to seek their favour, the priest sacrifices a chicken and beseeches the spirits of lightning, water and earth, as well as certain other local deities, to ward off any danger to the young crops in the fields.

There are two other gods, respectively called Ui-kasang and Nia-kasang, who are associated with war. Before raids, they were propitiated with the sacrifice of a dog, pig or bison to give courage and strength to the warriors. Another two deities (Pila and Yachu) are believed to help captives in escaping from the clutches of their enemies. On learning that an inhabitant of the village had been captured, a fowl was sacrificed inside the house, and invoking Pila and Yachu, the priest requested them to assist the captive in escaping. Similarly, when it was suspected that a bison had been stolen, the same deities were requested to enable the animal to escape by breaking its ties.

OPPOSITE AND FOLLOWING PAGE: *A priest preparing to sacrifice the* mithan.

On some occasions, the Apa Tani address the gods directly, but generally the priest is required to mediate between the world of the gods and human beings. A priest is not only the person through whom the gods and spirits speak, but as Furer-Haimendorf (1980:172) writes, "he is the repository of the tribe's sacred lore". He is expected to recite and chant for hours, invoke the gods, and narrate the relevant mythological events. The priest, then, is not simply someone who is selected by the gods and spirits to worship, but should ideally be a person gifted with excellent memory and a "sweet" voice. Novices are first attached to an experienced priest. Along with learning how to perform rituals and recite traditional chants, a priest is also expected to acquire the ability to enter *Neli*, the netherworld of supernatural powers and departed souls,

The Apa Tani believe that the netherworld is exactly like the world of living beings, except that it is free of suffering. In the netherworld, too, the people work, grow crops and perform rituals to appease the gods and spirits. Every woman who dies after her husband, goes to live with him in the netherworld, and vice versa. It is also believed that those who die unmarried find a spouse in neli and have children. The priests visit this world in their dreams; those who are especially gifted in memorising sacred lore can do so even when awake.

Besides the idea of the netherworld, the Apa Tani also believe in the another land of the dead (*talimoko*) in the sky. Those who die an unnatural death — men killed by wild animals or enemies, or women who die in childbirth, for example — end up here. The dead souls of the netherworld or the sky are believed to visit the world of the living, but such visits are not welcome. If a beautiful woman dies during childbirth, the Apa Tani say that her death was caused by a man from the sky who, having fallen in love with her, decided to take her to his world. Fearing these visits, the people ask the priest to perform sacrifices and request the departed souls stay away from the living world. The spirits of the netherworld may also come and cause illness and the priests perform sacrifices to prevent these visits as well.

OPPOSITE PAGE: *The priest's assistant.*

The mithan's *owners bring the animal to the place of sacrifice.*
OPPOSITE PAGE: *After the sacrifice, the* mithan's *flesh will be distributed to all the villagers.*

In recent years, with the spread of Christian, Buddhist and Hindu ideas, traditional Apa Tan views of the afterlife have been weakened. Many Apa Tani children now study in mission schools. Although not many in Subansiri district have adopted Christianity, the ideas of heaven and hell are now widespread. As a consequence, traditional ideas are being increasingly questioned.

Compared to the tribes of central India, the Apa Tani have made substantial progress. One of the reasons for this is that they were protected by a government policy, which did not allow people from the plains to settle in hill areas that were chiefly populated by tribal groups. In education, the Apa Tani have made impressive strides. Those who are educated, have entered into government service both at the central and state levels. Educated families invest a large proportion of their resources in sending their children to good schools in Assam and neighbouring states. It is hoped that the next generation of Apa Tani will be still better qualified and that their representation at both the state and central level will increase.

The sacrifice of the mithung.
OPPOSITE PAGE: *Sacrifice of a bird.*

KEYS TO
BEAUTY

The lands the tribes of India inhabit are beautiful and their arts and crafts mirror and enhance this beauty. Their jewellery is exquisite, and so are their costumes, and it is incredible that people who are dependent on the simplest technology have been able to create unique works of art and craft. Their wood-carvings and line drawings are extremely impressive, and their tattoo designs demonstrate a sophisticated and imaginative sense of elaboration.

Like all human societies, the tribes of India decorate their bodies. According to them, adorning the body is not simply a way of attracting others, but a means of respecting tribal customs. It is this that makes one feel "good" and "happy". The Rabari, for instance, say that, "A dishevelled person looks unhealthy and ghostly, and the woman whose hair is not bound invites evil spirits to possess her". Decorations raise the body from its natural and inauspicious state by investing it with culture and morality. Here we may refer to the Bonda belief that: "Beauty is not in the body, but in its ornaments. All bodies are fundamentally alike, we can make them different."

A Bhil man at Rishabdeo (Rajasthan).
OPPOSITE PAGE: *A young Bhil woman (Rajasthan).*

A Bonda bronze earring (Orissa)
PAGE 224: *Bonda necklaces consisting of coloured paste glass beads and five and ten paise coins (Orissa).*
PAGE 225: *A Rabari woman (Kutch, Gujarat).*

Gold nose rings of the Kuttia Kandha (Orissa).
BELOW: *Dang Bhil nose rings made of silver and stone (Gujarat).*

PAGE 228:
TOP LEFT & RIGHT: *Bonda necklaces (Orissa).*
MIDDLE LEFT: *Silver bells of the Kandha.* MIDDLE RIGHT: *A Bonda cap made of glass pearls.*
BOTTOM LEFT: *Anklets of the Rabari.* BOTTOM RIGHT: *Rabari silver necklaces*

PAGE 229: *Bonda woman dressed in all her jewellery, which is made from pearls, gold, silver and cloth.*
PAGE 230-231: *Saurashtrian women on their way to the Tarnetar Fair (Gujarat).*

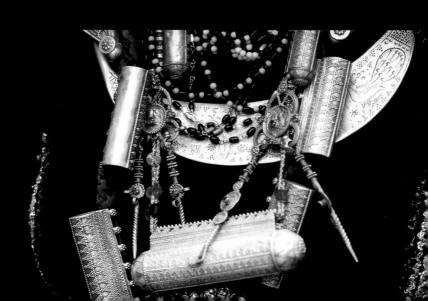

HIDDEN TRIBES OF INDIA

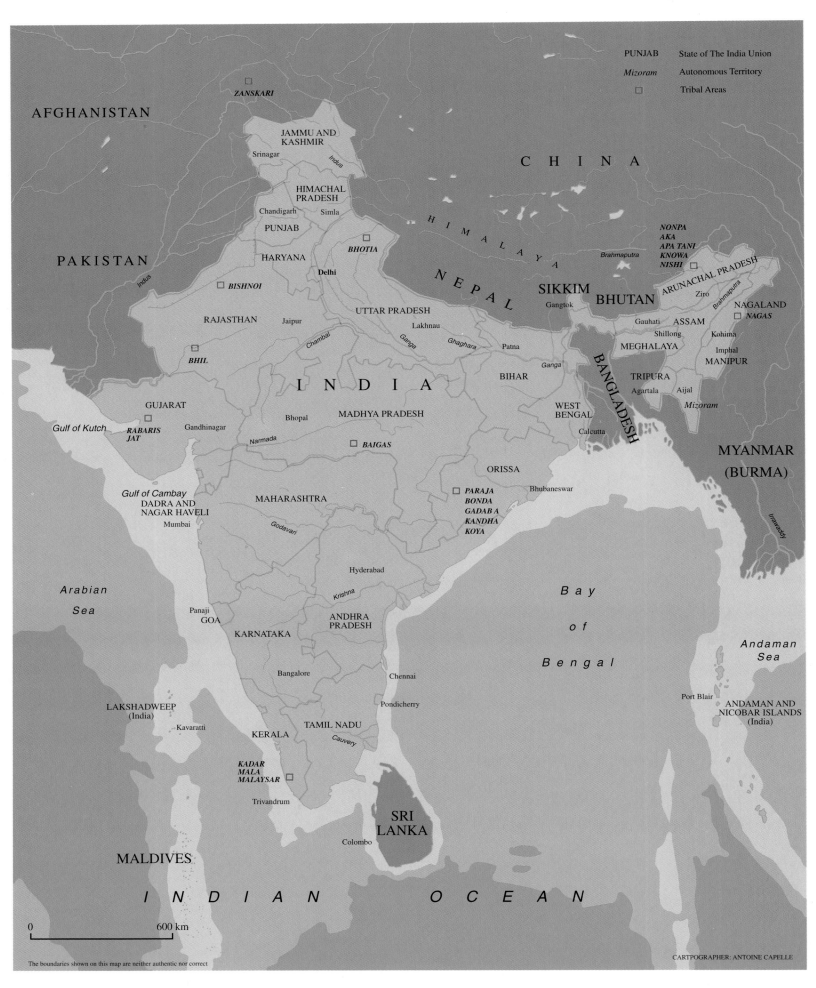

Original title: L'INDE DES TRIBUS OUBLIÉES
Written by: Declan Quigley – Vinay Srivastava
Photographs by: Tiziana and Gianni Baldizzone
Published by: Les Editions du Chêne-Hachette Livre 1993

Copyright © 1993, Editions du Chêne - Hachette Livre
English edition Copyright © 2000, Local Colour Limited,
Hong Kong
Colour separations by Intégral a Paris

Printing by Impression Couleurs Weber SA a Berne
Binding by AGM a Forges-les-Eaux
Art Director Philippe Pierrelée assisted by Sophie Domenach
Editors Marie Renault and Jonathan Griffin

ISBN 962-8711-03-02